SEEDS

—— OF ——

SUCCESS

PRAISE FOR *SEEDS OF SUCCESS*

"*Seeds of Success* belongs in the hands of every one of your sales and leadership team members. I believe the lessons in it could dramatically transform the way you do business."

—*Tip Fairchild, Director of Business Development, CleanBrands LLC, and Pitcher, Houston Astros*

"*Seeds of Success* is a fabulous read for leaders in any field, whether they are executives, athletes, coaches, or educators. It is every bit as much about the protégé as it is the mentor. As a professional in the executive search field, I can tell you Coach Bru has created a captivating story with profound lessons on talent management and human capital."

—*Ken Lubin, Managing Director of ZRG Partners and Founder of Executive Athletes*

"John has written an inspiring and entertaining story where you will learn key lessons about what it takes to be a top performer. You'll not only learn about sales and leadership; you'll also learn about yourself."

—*Jeff Beals, Professional Speaker and Author of the award-winning book* Selling Saturdays

"In my position helping companies meet the professional development needs of their employees, I'm always looking for the individual who can lead others through the process of awareness and practice that it takes to develop leadership. John Brubaker's latest book, *Seeds of Success*, will guide readers along their own path to becoming a truly effective leader."

—*Karina Drumheller, Manager of Professional Development and Training, University of New Hampshire*

"As I read this book, I swore parts of it were about me. John understands that an interesting story has to be about the reader, and he delivers. This story will make you pick up and call the one person that impacted you more than anyone else—your coach."

—*Colby B. Jubenville, PhD, Principal, Red Herring Innovation and Design*

"As an entrepreneur and a longtime coach, I speak from experience when I tell you this book transcends sport. The leadership and sales principles John shares are timeless and span all industries. Your personal library is incomplete without this book."

—*Chris Parisi, CEO, Turf Dawg USA*

"John's years of college coaching experience have real applications for business, sales, and leadership professionals. This is a brilliant story that will stick with you forever and, more importantly, affect your professional and personal life in a meaningful way. It's a must-read if you're serious about living a successful life."

—*Dan Tudor, President, Tudor Collegiate Strategies*

"In business and sports, too often we are focused on wins and losses. What get overlooked are the process and the leadership behind it. In *Seeds of Success* Coach Bru gives you a leadership game plan to build a culture of team synergy and excellence for your business, team, or family."

—*Dr. Rob Bell, Sport Psychology Coach and author of* The Hinge *and* Mental Toughness Training for Golf

"John has written a very touching and powerful story that will help you become the best version of yourself and bring out the best in your people. This book is life changing!"

—*Adam Todd, Principal, ADT Clinical Research*

"Winning in any industry requires exceptional leadership and communication skills, precisely the stuff John talks about in *Seeds of Success*. I highly recommend it!"

—*Jimmy Oliver, Manager of Business Development, LaxPower.com*

"If you want your leadership to grow to greatness, leave a legacy and live a more fulfilled life, buy this book."

—*Jeff Andrulonis, President/CEO of Colonial Media and Entertainment*

"Read this book, and you'll feel like you are taking a walk together on the fields of life with Jack and Coach Randall. You will learn about a great example of a leader as well as see a path to become one."

—*Terry Gobble, Director, Globe Union Services, Inc.*

"Wow! *Seeds of Success* will inspire you to use every minute more effectively! Leadership, self-development and team building are brought out in easy-to-apply steps! So many rush to the harvest; those who apply and use the *Seeds of Success* will have bountiful forever harvests. Read this book, share it with your team members and build forever harvests!"

—*Adam Arens, Owner, Patriot Subaru*

SEEDS

— OF —

SUCCESS

Leadership, Legacy, and Life Lessons Learned

JOHN BRUBAKER

NEW YORK

Seeds of Success
Leadership, Legacy, and Life Lessons Learned

Request for permission should be made in writing to:

John Brubaker
The Sport of Business, LLC
51 Waters Edge Dr.
Lewiston, ME 04240

Published in New York, New York, by Morgan James Publishing. Morgan James and The Entrepreneurial Publisher are trademarks of Morgan James, LLC.
www.MorganJamesPublishing.com

The Morgan James Speakers Group can bring authors to your live event. For more information or to book an event visit The Morgan James Speakers Group at www.TheMorganJamesSpeakersGroup.com.

Morgan James Publishing
The Entrepreneurial Publisher
www.MorganJamesPublishing.com

bitlit

A **free** eBook edition is available
with the purchase of this print book.

CLEARLY PRINT YOUR NAME ABOVE IN UPPER CASE
Instructions to claim your free eBook edition:
1. Download the BitLit app for Android or iOS
2. Write your name in **UPPER CASE** on the line
3. Use the BitLit app to submit a photo
4. Download your eBook to any device

9781630474973   paperback
9781630474997   eBook

Library of Congress Control Number:

Cover Design by:
3 Dog Design
www.3dogdesign.net
chris@3dogdesign.net

Interior Design by:
Brittany M. Bondar
www.Sage-Words.com

Habitat for Humanity®
Peninsula and
Greater Williamsburg
Building Partner

DEDICATION

To Randy and Marylyn Mills.

Your vision and ability to see people for what they can become
rather than what they are continues to inspire me. It's a lesson
I've put to use with the many young men I have coached and
one I will forever continue to use as a father and husband.

CONTENTS

PREFACE

This book is a work of fiction about a man named Jack Burton, whose career path was in many ways similar to my own. He thought he had all the answers but came to realize that we are all students and everyone we meet has a lesson to teach.

Burton sets out on a quest for knowledge to become a better coach, teacher, and person. Through the guidance of an unlikely mentor, Jack meets three extraordinary teachers and learns how creating a philosophy and having a system give you the power to access greater results in any endeavor.

Following the seeds of success that were planted for Jack will enable you to create game-changing breakthroughs in your life as well. I know this because they are lessons that have transformed mine.

The leadership lessons I am sharing with you are delivered as a story chronicling Jack's journey coaching lacrosse alongside his mentor, coaching icon Morgan Randall. The journey of the protégé and his mentor reflects this progression and demonstrates the profound influence a mentor can have in transforming the way people go on to coach, train, and lead others later in life.

College lacrosse, unlike other levels of lacrosse, is a year-long commitment. The season begins at the start of the academic year, has a winter off-season, and concludes with a spring season. Of the 40-plus players on a team, ten are on the field at any one time: three attack players, three midfielders, three defenders, and a goalie. College lacrosse is played on large outdoor fields and entails considerable physical contact.

A number of years ago, I was training to be a psychologist, chasing a dream that wasn't completely my own and thinking this was to be my career path. As I completed my residency, I began coaching to relieve the stress associated with being in an intense doctoral program. As I worked harder and got closer to the finish line, the goal posts seemed to move.

The day after I completed my second internship, I woke up, looked in the mirror, and came to the realization that I wasn't the same person I was when I began. I was stressed out, unhappy, and unfulfilled. As I looked ahead, I couldn't envision a career, much less a lifetime, of sitting in an office listening to other people's problems. It was at this time that I met my mentor and caught the coaching bug. As our season together evolved, I began to feel a gravitational pull taking my career in a new direction. Looking back, it's a direction for which I am very grateful.

The various strategies and tools you are about to learn are battle-tested and have withstood the test of time. To be precise, 42 years of a mentor helping hundreds of young men learn and understand the business of winning.

Don't just read this book; apply its lessons and teach them to others. Psychiatrist William Glasser determined that we learn 10 percent of what we read, 20 percent of what we hear, 30 percent of what we see, 50 percent of what we see and hear, 70 percent of what we discuss, 80 percent of what we experience, and 95 percent of what we teach others.

It's my hope that you will share *Seeds of Success* with people you care about. Teach them how applying these lessons can help them achieve game-changing results in their own lives and lead their team to the next level of excellence.

Thank you for allowing me to share *Seeds of Success* with you. I wish you a life where you help coach people to become their best.

ACKNOWLEDGEMENTS

Seeds of Success is a project that has been brought to life thanks to the efforts of some very talented, special people. I have always said that great teams have great teammates. I am profoundly grateful to my great teammates, mentors, and colleagues who have helped transform this book from vision to reality.

In 1996 I threatened to write a book chronicling my journey with my coaching mentor when we worked together. In a way it has finally happened. My only regret is that he is not here to read it. Special gratitude goes out to the Randy Mills family who has always treated me like one of their own.

I would also like to thank my publisher Morgan James Publishing, my editorial team of Paula Keeney and Ann Whetstone at Communications Ink, along with Paul Weaver whose coaching and eye for detail helped make this book shine.

I would like to extend a special acknowledgement to Major John Caldwell, Assistant Chief of Staff/National Director, Public Affairs, Marine Corps Recruiting Command, Quantico, Virginia, for sharing his insights on recruitment.

I owe a special thank you to mentors Jon Gordon, Jeff Andrulonis, and Peter Scott who have helped me take my game to the next level. You each, in your own way, remind me that we are all students and everyone has a lesson to teach us in life. Your example and coaching changed my life.

A big thank you goes out to Brian Cain for teaching me the concept of "walking on water." Another big thanks to Dr. Kevin Elko for introducing me to the scripture Philippians 4:8 through his teachings. And a very special thanks to Reverend Peter Mills for the metaphor of passing the baton. The reference to license plate LAX-22 is a tribute to my first high school coach, John Distler, who saw me for who I could become, not merely who I was at the time. You taught me the power of showing someone you believe in them when they didn't believe in themselves.

Lastly, I would like to thank my late father, Lt. Col. Thomas F. Brubaker, who was a living, breathing embodiment of mental toughness and leadership. Your example continues to inspire me to persevere through adversity.

1

A SEED PLANTED

It was meant to be just another workout. A three-mile jog around the Burlington County Park athletic field followed by a dozen wind sprints and finished up with a hundred shots on the lacrosse goal. It was the standard workout I had performed variations of for the past 10 years. The solitude of training in the country was a welcome change of pace from the pressure-packed days of graduate school and the stress of the daily commute into Philadelphia.

Lacrosse was the perfect outlet for me in high school and college, and now I just couldn't let go of the discipline of being a student-athlete. I was never considered the Michael Jordan of lacrosse, but I certainly was a student of the game. It was my first true love and always would be.

The game centered me and grounded me in a way nothing else could. When everything else in the world was going crazy or going wrong around me, the lacrosse field was the one constant in my life where everything went right. The world didn't make a whole lot of sense to me except on the lacrosse field.

Little did I know an unexpected visitor was about to plant a seed in my head that would quickly change everything.

"Hey, what's up? My name's Ben. Mind if I join you and shoot around a little bit?" the stranger asked as he walked onto the field, duffel bag in hand.

"Not at all, Ben. I've been coming here every evening at this time, 6 days a week for the past 2 years, and you're the first person I've seen."

"Yeah, it's a well-kept secret," replied Ben, smiling. "Let's try to keep it that way."

I didn't quite know what to make of this lanky, 6-foot kid with bleached blonde hair and a headband. He looked, sounded, and dressed more like a surfer dude than a lacrosse player. With his board shorts, tank top, and sweatband on his head, he could have passed for a product of the seventies.

"You've got some sweet lacrosse equipment there. Play competitively?" I asked.

"Yeah, I head back to college in a few days, so I'm just trying to work myself back into playing shape before I have to report for preseason training," he answered.

"Where do you play?"

"Oh, it's a little Division III college you probably never heard of," Ben said, somewhat sheepishly.

"Try me, Ben. I'm a fountain of obscure facts."

"Uh, Radnor University, it's on the . . . "

Before the stranger could complete the sentence, I blurted out, ". . . west end of the city. Of course I've heard of Radnor."

"Wow, Jack. I'm impressed. How'd you know Radnor? We ain't known for much," Ben replied.

"Probably the only way anyone has heard of that little school, Ben, is because Morgan Randall coaches lacrosse there. He started that team from scratch just a couple of years ago, and you guys have built a real solid program," I responded.

"Yeah, Coach is a living legend. Don't know that I have a whole lot to do with 'the build.' I'm really just a role player. Of course, Coach says everyone is a role player. It's one of his edges," Ben said.

"His what?" I asked.

"Oh yeah, sorry," Ben said. "Coach has a list of things, things that our program does differently than others, that sort of work as competitive edges over the opposition. At the end of practice each day he shares one edge to remind us who we are and what we're about. Some of the rookies think these are just little things, but little things make a big difference. When you add 'em up, there's your winning edge. At least that's what Coach says."

Now I was becoming intrigued with Ben's "Coach." For years I had known about Morgan's reputation as a highly regarded tactician and an elder statesman of the game, but I'd never gotten a behind-the-scenes look like this.

"I couldn't agree with Coach's philosophy more! Send me a schedule when you get back to school, and if it doesn't interfere with my team's schedule, I'll come check out a game. I'd love to meet your coach."

Ben jumped in quickly asking, "Wait a minute, Jack, what team do you coach around here?"

I was a bit embarrassed. "It's just a middle school team," I explained. "It's my way of giving back to the game, but I'd love to coach at a higher level someday. You know, maybe high school."

Ben got really animated. "Jack, someday might be today. We just got word that our assistant coach left to take a head coaching gig over at Valley Forge State College. You should give Coach a call. He loves to have a young, energetic assistant on staff. I know you'd get a ton of valuable experience, and just think, you'd get to learn from a legend."

The gears started turning in my head. I knew it could be an incredible learning experience. Kind of like an MBA candidate getting to serve as Warren Buffett's assistant at Berkshire-Hathaway. Coach Randall had probably built as many successful teams as Buffett had successful companies.

"I won't bug you about it anymore, Jack," Ben said. "Just tell me you'll at least think about it. Maybe give him a call. Mention my name, and tell him we spoke," Ben insisted.

"Well, when you put it that way, okay. Hey, it's worth exploring. Now, can we get back to shooting the ball? I mean that's what we came here to do, right?"

Ben was a man of his word and didn't say another word about Coach during the 90-minute shoot-around that turned into a game of one-on-one, with a few coaching pointers thrown in. His silence didn't really matter. The seed was planted and my mind was racing about this great opportunity.

We finished up our game and agreed to meet each evening at the same time until he headed back to school.

2

THE RECRUITING CALL

The next day, after a night of tossing and turning, I got up before the sun, fired up the coffee pot, and began drafting a cover letter to accompany a makeshift coaching résumé. As I typed furiously, I could hear my father's stern voice, "Son, if you're really interested in working for this guy, for God's sake don't tell it to him in a letter. I didn't fax the Air Force my résumé with a note telling them I wanted to enlist. I marched down to the recruiting station. And I sure as heck didn't propose to your mother by mailing her a letter."

While I had heard this story hundreds, maybe thousands, of times growing up, the message still rang true. Important things need to be done directly. And with that I picked up the phone and began dialing.

A rough voice on the other end said, "Coach here!"

I stumbled over my introduction. "Hello, Coach Randall, my name is Jack Burton."

The coach jumped in right away, "You a midfielder, Jack?"

"Uh, no. I'm actually not a student-athlete, sir. I am calling to speak to you about your assistant coaching position."

"Dadgummit, I'm looking for a lefty midfielder, about 6'2" and 200 pounds, who can shoot the lights out of the ball. You know anyone who fits the bill, Mack? Oh, and good grades. He's gotta be a serious student. Can't be a knucklehead either, character counts around hee-ah," the coach explained with a heavy Long Island accent.

"It's Jack, my name's Jack. Sorry Coach, I can't think of anyone off the top of my head. I'll let you know if I see one though."

"Well, if you want to work for me, you're gonna need an eye for talent," Randall shot back.

After a few minutes of exchanging the usual pleasantries and then sharing background information, I had gotten my foot far enough in the door for Coach to invite me for an interview the following afternoon.

3

BRAND **YOU**

As I pulled up to the field house the next day, my Honda Prelude was nearly run off the road by a madman zipping around the corner in a charcoal grey Ford Escort. The car had enough decals plastered all over it to make a NASCAR driver envious. Upon closer review, I noticed the decals were all lacrosse related. A Nike swoosh, a Spartan logo with crossed sticks, equipment manufacturers like Brine, Warrior, and STX all occupied space on virtually every panel of the car. Smack dab in the middle of his bumper was a sticker that read "Sticks and stones won't break your bones but a cross check to the ribs just might." I thought to myself, uh oh, this had to be the coach.

"Good, you're early!" Coach shouted as I stepped out of my car. "Early is on time, on time is late, and late loses you games. I tell my kids that, but they don't usually believe it 'til it happens to them. Sometimes kids today are a little too into that 'experiential learning.' You know what I mean?"

It looked like a sporting goods store had exploded inside his car. As he emerged from the vehicle, I wasn't sure if this man was crazy or crazy like a fox. He was dressed like the stereotypical old school coach: Bike brand coach's shorts, a grey t-shirt that read "Property of Radnor University Athletics," and black sneakers with bleach white laces. With his sense of humor, silver hair, sly grin, and sparkle in his eyes, he could have passed for Rodney Dangerfield's stunt double for sure.

I greeted the coach as he extended a hand, "Hi, Coach. Jack, Jack Burton. It's good to meet you."

"Glad to meet you, too, number 22," Coach said with a sly grin.

"How'd you know that was my number in college?"

"I might be old, but I ain't blind, Mack. Read it on your license plate—LAX-22. From the looks of that, we're gonna get along famously. You see, I'm a big believer in advertising. Promote the sport. It's our product. More importantly, promote your personal brand."

"Personal brand?" I said, a little confused.

"I guess you never heard of the McDonald's Theory, huh?" he countered.

"Can't say that I learned that in grad school," I replied, shaking my head.

"Why do you think McDonald's has served billions of hamburgers? Because they're so healthy and good for you? Heavens no! Because it advertises everywhere. Same thing with my car. I wanna be a billboard on wheels for Radnor University. Every high school game, recruiting showcase, and any other pit stops I make, people will know the ole coach is in the house. Making those brand impressions has been especially important for us as a relatively new program."

As we made our way across campus, I learned in short order that Coach was a master at differentiating his brand. From the bright green argyle blazer and white suede shoes he wore on the road recruiting to his voicemail greeting recorded by what sounded to be an attractive co-ed, lacrosse gear displayed all over campus, and his famous "pope-mobile" as the kids called it. His preferred method of transportation around campus was via his personal golf cart, custom-built for him by a booster.

It was probably nicer than most people's cars. It was painted Radnor blue, gold, and white, had glass windows on all sides, and probably the only thing missing was an espresso machine. On this day he used it to show me around campus, but usually he used it to drive recruits around. What a not-so-subtle differentiator and status symbol! How many recruits got driven around campus in the coach's personalized golf cart at the other colleges they visited? I would venture to say none, and I'm sure Coach found a way to slide that in during their campus tours.

"McDonald's Theory. Smart thinking, Coach. You're right. Its advertising is unavoidable. I never looked at it that way before. How else do you differentiate yourself?"

"Well, it's not differentiating me, but it certainly shines a huge spotlight on the program. Does that count?"

"Sure, Coach. What is it?"

"Jack, would you believe me if I told you little ole Radnor lacrosse is the most widely watched amateur sporting event in the entire state?"

By now, I was starting to think he might be a little over the top, even for me (and that was saying a lot).

"No way. That I'd find hard to believe."

"Well, prepare to be amazed, my young friend. See that satellite dish over there on the hilltop?"

"Over there by the communications building? Yeah, I see it. What about it?"

"We've got a small broadcast journalism program in the communications department, along with a public access television studio. Usually they just videotape monthly city council meetings, some boring chamber of commerce event, lighting of the Christmas tree, stuff like that. The rest of the time, which is most of the time, there's just a scrolling community billboard listing area events. Well, I convinced Ozzy, that's what I call Professor Osborne who heads up the department, to videotape our games."

"I get it, so you could have game film to break down and show the team, right?" I said, realizing this guy just might have a method to his madness.

"Well, that's the obvious part, and we do use it as a teaching tool for our current players. That was part of my motivation, but the bigger part was to create a buzz about our program in the community. Here's the deal. Two broadcast journalism majors get internship credit for doing the color commentary and play-by-play of all our games. One of the video production students gets the same deal for producing our highlight film each year."

"That sounds good, but how does that make you the most-widely watched amateur sporting event in the entire state? I mean Penn State has a pretty good football following outside of State College."

"A couple of Penn State's games air nationally, but the rest are just televised locally. Our games, going back to that satellite dish up there on the hill, get sent via satellite feed to every public access channel in every town and city across the entire state of Pennsylvania. And the best part is that it's free!"

"How on earth did you negotiate that, Coach? Do you have an agent?" I asked in absolute amazement.

"No negotiation necessary," he laughed. "Remember I told you there wasn't enough interesting programming to air on public access stations, so stations just run that boring scrolling community billboard? Well, I hope you don't think that's unique to Radnor. Every community in the state has the same problem, not enough manpower to produce local content. I just gift-wrapped them a solution. Our lacrosse games air on 54 different stations in every corner of the state. That's 53 more markets than that Division I football team you mentioned."

"Amazing, Coach. How do you leverage that?"

"Really, Jack, it just leverages itself. I just make sure when I'm scheduling home visits with recruits that I schedule them for the same time our game is being shown on their stations."

"Let me guess. When you visit them, you make sure they turn their TV on and see the team playing while you're sitting in their living room."

"Bingo! You guessed it, Jack. That's the leverage. The funniest part of the whole deal is that there are four other colleges we compete against who have the same resources we do, and their local station airs our games, not theirs, because their coach never bothered to approach 'em about it."

"Coach, that's amazing and hilarious, but I kind of actually feel bad for those coaches. They either aren't creative enough to think of how to market their programs or they aren't motivated enough to ask the station."

"Jack, don't feel bad for them. It's their own fault. Did you know John F. Kennedy's nanny didn't vote for him years later when he ran for president of the United States?"

I thought for sure that Coach was pulling my leg this time and wondered what this had to do with anything. "What? No way!!" I said skeptically.

Getting defensive, Coach replied, "No, really. You can look it up. He asked her later who she voted for, and when she said 'not you,' he asked why. Her answer was simply, 'I would have but you never asked me to.' You see, Jack, just like Kennedy, these other coaches did that to themselves; they didn't ask. I did. All it takes is asking. You ask often enough, and you will find the right people."

I needed to start writing down this stuff. As I took out my notebook, I got to thinking that Coach was making great points about marketing and branding. So I wrote down the following: "You will always get 100 percent of what you don't ask for, but if you only get 30 percent or 40 percent of what you do ask for, you're still far better off."

I could already see that I was going to have an interesting day (in a good way) and maybe learn some useful things.

"Coach, those are fantastic stories, both about JFK and your television coverage."

"Don't worry, kid. There's plenty more where that came from. You can either read my book or see my movie!" Coach said, giving me a wink. As he parked the golf cart in front of his office, he asked, "Are you ready to talk some lacrosse?"

4

LITTLE TESTS

We made our way into the administration building. I could see my reflection in the door as we passed through and realized my tie was crooked, so I scrambled to adjust it, buttoned my blazer, and hoped Coach hadn't noticed. I wondered what the coach's office would look like, where I should sit, and what his first question might be. I began to feel in over my head and grossly underprepared. At least I was dressed appropriately, I thought. That ought to count for something.

I was expecting Randall's office to look like a lawyer's with leather furniture and a big mahogany desk. Hardly. His office was an oversized cubicle in the corner of the admissions department. The desk looked like someone had organized it with a leaf blower. The walls were a walk down memory lane, covered with team photos and award plaques. His bookshelf was filled with history books and books written by every military leader from Sun Tzu to General Norman Schwarzkopf.

The moment we sat down, Coach caught me eyeing the surroundings and broke the ice by saying, "Well, I know what you must be thinking. Not much of an office, huh? You coach 40 some years, earn a couple hundred wins, and your office is a cubicle in the basement of the campus center. I bet a lot of other schools you've been to the coaches had real nice offices, real good-lookin' furniture."

He paused for a moment and looked me right in the eye. "I bet you it was kind of intimidating. Man, I didn't want an office like that, you know. I didn't want a palace. I wanted a place where you could just come right in and sit down. The kind of place where you could put your feet up on the desk, and there was an atmosphere of honesty and trust. I think that's the type of relationship a coach has with his assistant and with his players. There has to be a feeling of trust there. I mean, I want you to be able to walk through that door and feel that you can share anything with me."

Hearing him say that made me think here is a man who despite all his accomplishments hasn't let success go to his head. He wasn't too impressed with himself, and above anything he valued relationships. This intense second impression overrode my first impression of nearly getting run off the road.

I'd have to keep wondering what his first question might be though. Coach Randall shouted, "Follow me" and made an about-face for the front door and headed back outside toward the stadium.

I couldn't have, in a million years, anticipated the first interview question being what it was . . . "So Jack, ya' ever lined a field before?"

"No, Coach, can't say I have."

"Well, today is your lucky day. You get to learn from the master. I've been doing this so long that when I first started coaching Christ was just a teenager," he laughed. "He made a lousy defenseman, wouldn't hit anyone."

As we left the administration building and headed down to the stadium, I took another look at my reflection in the glass double doors and felt a little different on the way out than on the way in. I was now more than a tad overdressed. So I took off my jacket and tie and began to roll up my sleeves to get to work. There was nothing quite like the smell of fresh-cut Bermuda grass and field paint to stir up the memories of one's college days. Although I'd never lined a field, my work-study job in college was field maintenance, so I felt right at home, sort of.

To call this facility a stadium was being generous at best. It was more like a glorified pasture surrounded by bleachers. I was used to playing my games in a legitimate football stadium that seated a few thousand under the lights on a Saturday night.

Coach was surprisingly quiet as we set the strings and stakes to square the perimeter of the field. His lines were a little loose, and we ran out of paint. But, other than that, it went pretty smoothly.

He asked relatively few questions and then listened intently. The questions felt a little like the first couple of punches a prizefighter throws in the early rounds to see what the other guy is made of. There were just four. At the time it seemed coincidental that they were asked one per side as we lined the perimeter. Coach led with, "Why do you want to be a college coach?" Then as we started to tackle the next part of the field, he asked, "What makes you different from other coaches?" About halfway he caught me off guard asking, "What do you do better than anyone else?" Then just before we finished putting the goals back in their proper places, he looked up and said, "Tell me why I should hire you, Jack?"

I made sure my answers came from the heart yet at the same time were measured. As we put the finishing touches on the goal lines and returned the equipment to the field house to clean up, Coach extended his hand and gave me a hearty handshake, saying, "The job is yours if you want it. The pay is lousy and the hours are long, but the rewards are priceless."

I'm sure my expression let him know I was more than a little surprised to get an immediate decision. I smiled and without hesitation said, "Count me in." With that, Coach, still clutching my hand with his oversized mitt, pulled me in and gave me a bear hug. "Welcome to the team, lookin' forward to working with you, partner. Let's meet up tomorrow morning at the office and get you a lay of the land."

Partner, I thought to myself . . . partner . . . I like the sound of that. The word partner had a real nice ring to it. Hopefully, we would be partners. The best jobs I've ever had were when I worked with someone as if we were business partners, not just working for them like a hired hand.

As I drove home, I replayed in my mind the entire interaction with Coach Randall. It struck me that perhaps the lining of the field wasn't as impromptu as I had initially thought. Given his experience and how perceptive he was, he probably used lining the field as a test of who I am and what I'm about. For someone who'd surely lined thousands of fields over the years, he did seem to set the stakes a little crooked and the strings a little loose. I bet he used that as a measuring stick to assess my attention to detail. Did I notice? Did I politely adjust the line, or did I just let shoddy work happen?

Then I thought that based on experience, he had to have known how much paint we needed to do the job. How could he run out of paint? I think he just wanted to see my reaction. I probably would have taken myself out of the opportunity if I hadn't volunteered to go get more.

I was a bundle of mixed emotions, excited and apprehensive at the same time. Either way, I was about to embark on an exciting journey.

5

REFLECTIONS

My mind was racing every bit as much as my car was on my morning commute to campus. I wondered what it would be like to work as an assistant to the great Morgan Randall. I knew he had a track record a mile long for getting his assistants head coaching jobs after their time with him. In just the past three years, his last three assistants landed highly coveted head coaching positions in the immediate area. Being a member of his coaching tree was obviously a great springboard to your career, and I'd be lying if I said this wasn't a huge part of my attraction to the job. I hadn't worked a minute for the man yet it felt like I was headed to work for lacrosse's equivalent of football coach Woody Hayes, who had mentored more assistants into head coaching jobs than any other coach of his era.

I knew I was putting the cart before the horse. It was nice to wonder but time to get back to reality. My thoughts turned to the office, if you could even call it that. It felt more like sitting in a phone booth. Having seen his humble workstation, I had my doubts if I'd even get an office. Maybe I'd have to share his cubicle, frightening thought. Would I even get a chair for that matter?

Ten minutes later, I arrived at the office to find a metal folding chair waiting for me. I guess that puts one question to rest, I thought to myself. Legal pad and pen in hand, I was armed with a list of questions a country mile long. After a cup of stale office coffee and some small talk, we downshifted and began talking strategy.

I immediately started asking questions. "Coach, what style offense and defense are we going to run this year?"

"Same one I run every year, partner," Coach quipped.

"Can I look at the playbook to get acquainted with the system?"

"Sure, it's gonna be the fastest read of your life, kid," Coach replied as he reached across the desk to hand me a distressed, ancient-looking navy blue leather three-ring binder with the Vegas gold Radnor Block R logo emblazoned on the cover. As I cracked the binder open and looked down, I knew I'd been had. The binder was filled with what looked to be about 100 pages, corners bent and practically a mustard yellow shade due to age. A hundred blank pages!

"Okay, Coach, very funny. But how am I going to learn the system if I can't study a playbook?"

Leaning in and putting his hand on my shoulder, Coach, in a most serious tone, softly said, "Plays don't win games. Players win games. Please always remember this. It's not the Xs and Os that win games. It's the Jimmys and Joes."

As I quickly wrote down his words, Coach followed up with, "At this point you're probably wondering what the heck we will spend our time doing if we don't have a playbook. We invest time in recruiting and teaching. By recruiting I mean hitting the road and by teaching I mean on the practice field. That's why you don't have your own office or desk. If you're doing the job right, trust me, you don't need either one."

"Makes sense now, Coach. I think I get what you mean. Can't wait to learn how you do both."

Coach explained that the problem with most teams is that the coaches overcoach and the players underprepare. The foundation of his program was to make sure that neither of those two things was allowed to happen. My newfound mentor swiftly reached up to his bookshelf and handed me his *Webster's Dictionary*. "Before you walk onto the practice field or walk into a recruit's living room, you need to embrace one simple concept. Look up these two words: coach and teach."

As the gears were turning in my head, I gave Coach an inquisitive look, smiled, and said, "What? Another book filled with blank pages?"

Stone-cold serious this time, he said, "Not quite. This is for real, look them up and write down the definitions." As I thumbed through the monstrosity of a dictionary, I was amazed by both Coach's and Webster's wisdom. The definitions were the same... "to provide instruction."

It was as if the proverbial light bulb went on in my head, to coach is to teach and to teach is to coach. One fed the other; they were synonymous. This was Coach's answer to the problem of over-coaching and underpreparing. If you can provide instruction in a way that makes something complex simple to the learner, he will execute better, respond faster, and learn more successfully. At this point, I knew the season was going to be an exciting, and proba-bly enlightening, ride.

"So I guess I understand why you don't have a playbook, but let me ask you this . . . The game is tied with less than a minute left on the clock; we gain possession of the ball and call time out. What do you tell the team in the huddle if you're not calling a play?"

"I wouldn't," he said very matter-of-factly.

"What do you mean by you wouldn't?" I asked.

Coach Randall took this question as an opportunity to have a teachable moment, something I soon learned he would always do. "For starters, we won't be calling time out. You give them time to set their defense and find the matchups they want. That's what 99 percent of the teams do, so everyone expects that to happen. Instead, we do the unexpected. If we've got one opportunity to win the game on one possession, I'm giving the ball to my best scorer and telling everyone else to get the heck out of his way."

"That's all you'd do?" I asked with some astonishment.

"Absolutely, Jack, absolutely. Here's why. If I did a better job recruiting than the other team's coach, then I can look myself in the eye and know with a fair amount of confidence that we're gonna win. That confidence is contagious when I talk to the players. They can sense it and buy in. Plus they know what's going on out there better than we do. They're living it, and we're just watching from the sidelines."

Still a little wary, I responded, "I believe you, Coach. I guess I'll have to see it in action to get that feeling myself."

Two weeks later in a fall tournament, wouldn't you know that exact situation arose in a game against Mountain Valley State. It was tied 8-8 with 16 seconds remaining. The officials awarded us the ball off a turnover, and sure enough, Mountain Valley's coach called time out. His assistant coach, Jay Dillon, had been a college teammate of mine. I thought I knew what he would do defensively in this situation, so I mentioned it to Coach before we huddled up with the team. "Coach, he's going to double-team whoever we have inbound the ball. It's what we did when we played together for four years in college."

Coach responded coolly, "It doesn't matter, Jack. I'm giving the ball to Joe, who's gonna beat his man and score. He's been beating the guy all day!" He turned, looked at a group of nervous players in the huddle, and said, "Two ducks walked into a bar. The first duck orders two beers, the second duck whispers, 'How are you going to pay?' 'It's all right,' says the first duck. 'I'll get him to put it on my bill.'"

This tactic was absolute genius. He took the pressure off of them and put it on to himself. It was a wonderful balance of competitive genius and boyish fun, the right words at the right time. After everyone had a good laugh and the tension was gone, he said, "Listen up! We're gonna win this game right now. Here's how we do it. Joe, you're gonna inbound the ball up top. You other five guys just need to get out of his way and create space for him to work."

Lo and behold, Joe inbounds the ball at midfield, splits the double team, and while driving to the goal, fakes a pass to the wing so convincingly the goalie moved out of position to defend it. With the clock ticking down to 5, 4, 3, 2 seconds, Joe shoots on a virtually empty net and puts home the game winner.

At that moment, Coach walked down the sideline, put his arm around me, and said, "Jack, now do ya' see why we don't complicate winning around here? Not in lacrosse, not in anything. It's real simple. We play to our strengths. Do what we do well, execute it better than anyone else, and we'll have success."

Little did I know how important those words would become to me. I'd learn that it's the same thing if you're running a company, a church, a military unit, or a household. You can't be worried about what the competition is doing; it takes your focus off the right things. Under pressure we tend to think we need to do more, when in reality we need to do less but do it perfectly.

That end-of-game situation was also a life lesson on the benefits of being a contrarian. In competition play to your strengths and do the unexpected so people are not prepared for what they're about to face.

When we returned to campus, I told Coach, "I'm not sure I'd have had the courage to put the game in Joe's hands without giving him any coaching."

"You will, Jack, but it comes with experience. Before you can effectively coach and teach, you need to develop a leadership philosophy. Don't worry. It won't be perfect right away; Lord knows I'm still not. Your leadership philosophy is something you'll wrestle with your entire career. Even at my age I still have to remind myself that the coach is the team and the team is the coach. You reflect each other. That's why I ask myself three simple questions at the beginning of each year:

1. Who am I? (In coaching terms)

2. What influence do I bring to this organization?

3. How much do I coach them versus turn them loose and really let them play?

"These answers will change a little for every leader each year, based on personnel and experience. So start asking yourself those questions."

"Okay, Coach, I'll start thinking and putting my thoughts on paper. It's going to take awhile though."

"Take all the time you need. It'll come to you. For now I want to go back to your original question about the playbook. While we might not have a playbook for you to study to get to know the players' strengths, we do have game film. You can start to get an idea of what these guys are all about by watching tape and spending time with them. I've got some meetings off campus, but I should finish up by the time you get through the film. At that point, we'll hit the road. I've got a couple recruits we need to visit this evening."

As he was walking out of the office, he called back to me, "By the way, ditch the tie, Jack, it makes you look uptight. Besides, you'll be overdressed for where we're going. The Central league is full of blue-collar kids from blue-collar families. Those are my kind of kids. The kind you can win with. I've always built my teams with a blue-collar mentality."

As I glanced over at the all-white game jersey on the wall, I realized it was no small coincidence that the only ounce of color other than the numbers was a thick navy blue band around the collar.

The lesson in Coach's three-question test was understanding that no matter how many years you're in the business, whatever business that may be, every year brings something new with a new cast of characters. The leader is the team, and the team is the leader. Yet you cannot be so set in your ways that you're unwilling to embrace change or reinvent yourself. Doing so could be the very thing to vault your program or your business to new heights.

6

WHICH ONE ARE YOU?

Each practice began and ended with a few words from Coach. They were always thought provoking and timely. Sometimes the message was born out of frustration; other times it was philosophical. But it always had a teaching point. Subtle or obvious, depending on the situation. On one occasion Coach opted to end practice with the obvious.

"Which one are you? Which one are you?" His voice reverberated through the aluminum stadium bleachers as he bellowed his question at the squad.

Todd, a senior captain, made the mistake of responding to Coach's rhetorical question. "Which what, Coach?"

His teammate Ben whispered into the ear hole of his helmet, "I don't think he was really looking for a response yet, dude."

"Which one are you? Are you a player or are you a pretender?" Coach asked again, following it with instructions to answer in their own heads.

"Let me help you. A player really goes for it in his own life. A pretender is a spectator in someone else's life.

"If you spend more time actually studying things, reading books, and listening to CDs to better yourself, to help you become a better person, you'll end up being the person you really want to be. And that's a player!" He deliberately paused to let the message sink in with his troops.

"If you waste your time watching TV, watching people be what they want to be, then you're a spectator. Stop wasting time watching TV. It's nothing more than watching other people being exactly what they want to be. Are you a player or a spectator?

"Every team I've led has had a couple people on the roster who'd rather act the part than do their part. They try to look the role, talk the role, and claim the role, but they always fall shy of filling the role. If I just described you, please know that you will either change or get exposed for who you are very quickly."

The metal bleachers creaked as several anxious players began shifting in their seats.

Coach continued, "Players have a servant's heart. Pretenders have a selfish heart. There are several players who are more talented than your captain Todd, here," he said, pointing to his captain in the back right-hand corner of the bleachers. "He was named one of your captains over them because he's worried about being the best player for the team; they're more worried about being the best players on the team. It's the difference between being mission conscious or position conscious."

Even after a few days, I knew Coach was right. Todd was the kind of player who never had to lobby to be named captain; he was too busy just making himself indispensable every day. This explained why he was named a captain and starter in just his sophomore year. Meanwhile some of his peers spent their time trying to move up the promotional ladder, so to speak. Coach called it "destination disease," meaning the grass is always greener on the other side of the fence. People suffering from this affliction can't seem to do the job they're in well enough but think they could do everything better if they were promoted to a position of authority like captain.

What got Coach started on this rant was the fact that he caught wind that a majority of the team members were in the student lounge the night before watching some Hollywood awards show instead of studying.

"Start watching and listening to people who can make you better, rather than people who just entertain you. We are stuck in an entertainment culture. Look at the Oscars and the Academy Awards. People spend days before and after the event analyzing it, watching other people walk the red carpet. These aren't even the award winners walking the carpet; they are just other entertainers."

The message began to be crystal clear to the team . . . be into education more than entertainment. Be into bettering yourself rather than just being a spectator of someone else who is bettering himself.

Coach quickly ended with a little empathy. "Sometimes it's hard not to be a spectator; it's hard not to be entertained. Hard is worthwhile though, because success is hard. Too many people look to be entertained and live through other people instead of achieving themselves. Successful people don't watch the news; they're too busy making the news. Understand this . . . you cannot hide in this program, you've got to be accountable and committed. You can't be a spectator."

He then reached into a large cardboard box at his feet and pulled out a navy blue t-shirt. "Each day during off-season workouts the staff will get together and judge your effort. We use a simple thumbs-up, thumbs-down system. If you get four thumbs-up, you get to wear a navy t-shirt the next day. Three thumbs-ups results in a white practice shirt. Two or less means you wear the dreaded yellow t-shirt. For you rookies, yellow is the color of our archrival Eastern State College."

The beauty of his system lay in its transparency and simplicity. When players report to workouts the next morning, their effort level is obvious to everyone. Everyone on the team knows what you did the day before and what your commitment to the team's goals was. Coach was always happy to point out the players wearing yellow and share a few choice words with them, but the message was clear—if you didn't like what you were wearing, all you had to do was change your effort.

Coach's message to the team was spot on. In life you really can't hide. Whether it's at work, at home, in the classroom, or on the field, your résumé is built every day. The colored shirts spoke to Coach's method of setting high expectations and holding players accountable.

As we began our walk back from the stadium to the office, I was filled with questions. "Coach, where did you get the idea for those color-coded t-shirts?"

"General George Crook once said 'Example is the best general order.' Our guys need to understand that how you show up is important. They've got to show up with a great attitude and great effort consistently. The shirts are a motivator to instill a burning desire to be successful. They've got to learn how to pay the price and do it with integrity and discipline.

"Did you see the way they were huddled around the TV in the locker room before practice?

"They could have been watching game film, they could have been reading, studying, doing anything to better themselves, but no, they were all huddled around the screen watching TMZ. After spending most of the evening doing the same thing from what I heard."

I had to admit that I'd seen the same things and was surprised.

Coach continued, "Now I'm not saying I never watch television, but the only shows I watch are on the History Channel because you can learn from history. History is a great educator, and success leaves clues, Jack. Be into education, not entertainment.

"I didn't come out and tell the guys this point blank, but we have too many people who are more concerned with looking the part than playing their part. You know a few of the characters I'm talking about. They're more concerned with wearing the jacket and all the gear, being big men on campus, and worrying about their position on the team, not the team itself. They only spell team with two of the letters: the M and the E. You can hear them coming a mile away 'cause when they speak, you'll hear 'em say me and I, not we and us."

I smiled. "Pretty sure I know who you're talking about, Coach. These guys definitely slow us down and can get us off track. We've gotta make sure we don't let their negativity spread in the locker room."

Coach met my observation with an assignment. "I'll put you in charge of that. The pretenders are all yours. Okay, partner? Otherwise I'll lose my mind with those maniacs; they think they know a better way. If something's not working, they want to change course instead of putting their nose to the grindstone. You can help them to focus on what's important. You've practically got a doctor's degree in rocket surgery or whatever you're in grad school for."

"Psychology, Coach. It's psychology," I tried to explain without laughing out loud.

"Even better, we've got a few mental patients on our hands. You guys ought to be a match made in heaven. Your goal is going to be to try to convert as many pretenders as you can into players. It takes patience, and I got news for you, don't be surprised if we lose a few on the way. But on the flip side, some of the younger guys with the right mentoring will turn into impact players."

"Well, Coach, if they don't figure it out now, they will when they graduate. Nothing works unless you do."

Coach nodded in agreement. "I'll just keep my eye on the impact players. They don't have that problem. They're my kind of guys. They'd play for free, wouldn't even need a field. They'd just show up, play you in the parking lot, and beat you. The funny thing is when you are a player, you don't care what position you play. Your position is called whatever will help the team."

"I'd like to think you and I were that kind of player, Coach. I don't know about you, but I was just happy to contribute wherever I could when I was playing," I said, thinking back to my own playing days.

"Same with me, Jack, but let's take it a step further. Would you believe me if I told you there's another even smaller population within the team? You'll get to meet them when we do our community service. The servants, they are the real impact players. Their role is to help their teammates be successful and help the less fortunate in the community, guys like Todd. You're probably getting an idea who some of the other guys are in practice; you'll figure out who all of them are when we do our Thanksgiving food drive for community service. For them it's all about the mission, being their best."

"I'm looking forward it. It's fascinating. I never realized before how you can learn about the guys on the field from what they do off the field."

"How you do anything is how you do everything, Jack. Why do you think I hired you?"

"Was it my charm and good looks, or did I dazzle you with my answers during the interview?" I joked.

"Well, you can rule out the first part of that statement, and I hate to break it to you but it sure wasn't your answers either. I watched how you lined that field with me. You took initiative, were willing to get your hands dirty, didn't accept my crooked lines at face value, and probably most importantly didn't try to take any shortcuts."

"Now I see what you mean about how you do anything is how you do everything, Coach. You mean to tell me lining that field was a setup? You were evaluating me even when I wasn't saying anything."

"That's right. It's how I know you're an impact player, Jack. You know, it's a funny thing. Over the years after they've graduated, you'll see that the impact players are the one's still competing. A lot of them have gone into coaching like you and me. I think they realize serving is just another way they can make an impact.

"Remember this when you're a head coach, Jack. Commitment as a team has to begin with individual leaders committing themselves to excellence before you can expect others to make that same commitment. You commit to setting a standard of excellence, and others will follow because they have to see your commitment for it to be contagious. Aspiring must always precede inspiring."

"I know what you mean, Coach. Leadership by example really sets a tone."

There was one thing that really bothered Coach: unrealized potential, wasted talent. When he saw players give less than their best or clown around in practice, he was bothered because they were wasting their talent and cheating themselves. He would tell the team he could deal with missed shots, dropped balls, and any other mistakes committed at full speed on the field. But what bothered him was when players cheated themselves.

I think he felt this way because lacrosse and the team were among the few things in his life. He had his family, and he had the team. Coach didn't have hobbies. He enjoyed reading murder mysteries and studying history in the evenings, but didn't have hobbies like golf, tennis, or collecting stamps to occupy him. Coaching was his passion. It was his vocation and avocation. He could deal with losing if the team gave its best effort. It was personal with Coach. It drove him nuts when players cheated themselves and the team by giving less than their best effort.

A championship effort that didn't result in a win was okay with Coach because of what it did for the players. It was so important to him because it made his players mentally tougher. So in anything they wanted to do after college they would be able to outcompete people around them because they had learned how pay the price, how to have a superior work ethic, courage in decision making, focus, intensity, commitment, and willpower. He understood that the skills you learn from athletics give you a better chance to succeed at life and have a competitive edge in the workplace. Skills like mental toughness, taking instructions, strategizing, and not being afraid of losing.

There is an art and a science to coaching, and I was beginning to see that Coach Randall had the unique ability to get his teams to perform in a number of ways. He could command, cajole; he could be cool, calm, and collected; and he could be angry. Any time he demonstrated one of these emotions, it was by design. Today's outburst was a perfect example of his strategic thinking. I was learning how he had an incredible grasp of how to use all kinds of psychological tools to bring out the best in people.

7

BUILDING THANKS

Team building was an everyday event with Coach, but this day the calendar flipped to November and team building took on new meaning. Each year for the past 40 years as the team entered the off-season, Randall took the opportunity to build each squad into a more closely knit group through a collective challenge while at the same time helping them realize their blessings. The challenge was organizing a Thanksgiving Food Drive for needy families in the community.

"Okay, partner, are you ready to see what this group is made of?"

"It's the off-season, Coach. We'll have to wait a couple months for that, won't we?"

Coach had me a little confused. We just wrapped up our 6-week non-traditional fall season and per NCAA rules we couldn't practice as a team again until February 1 when the official spring season began. All we could do was meet with them and encourage them to work out together. I didn't think we'd get to see what they were made of until February at the earliest.

"Nah, I'm not talking about on the field. I mean their leadership off the field. I learn just about everything I need to know about my guys every year at this time."

"How do you figure? It's just community service."

"Jack, it's way more than that. Just wait and see. You do good, and good will follow. They've been a group up until now. Some years they are nothing more than a collection of individuals at this point. After this activity, they always become a team."

"Okay, I'll suspend my judgment. What can I do to help organize this?"

"The best and most important thing you can do is nothing. It's what we both need to do, partner."

"What do you mean, Coach? I want to do my fair share of the work."

"You and I are the facilitators. We stay in the background and just make sure the fellas get out of their own way. Todd and the other two captains will delegate the responsibilities, handle the division of labor, and are in charge of accountability and execution from start to finish."

I laughed, "Sounds like good practice for when they start work."

For 2 weeks the entire team collected donations on and off campus to build awareness of the event. This year the team had tri-captains, and the three of them really took division of labor to a higher level, leaving no stone unturned in the process. They understood team building is about putting the right people in the right roles with the right goals. By doing so, you not only play to people's strengths but also allow their unique talents to shine.

Ben and the other business majors were charged with the responsibility of soliciting companies to sponsor the event. The marketing majors created flyers and positioned donation boxes in high-traffic areas around campus for people to drop off canned goods. They even thought to have the two health education majors on the team plan the menu to ensure it was balanced and had nutritional value. The week before Thanksgiving break the team was scheduled to deliver the baskets to a local food pantry.

Great leaders, leaders of significance, help grow other leaders. Our captains did so by enlisting the assistance of a local Boy

Scout troop to make Thanksgiving cards to accompany each food basket.

At the end of the fundraising campaign, the captains shopped for the Thanksgiving groceries. It was when they brought the supplies back to campus that the magic began. With the efficiency of a Detroit production line, the captains had the team assemble and package the baskets. Players on the roster who previously didn't get along were now rallying around the cause, building morale and good will. You could literally see the players embracing what Coach Randall called the four keys to successful team building.

1. **Shared Ownership.** Quite simply, they weren't just becoming a team. They realized it was "their" team.

2. **Shared Challenge.** Coach issued the challenge of identifying and feeding 48 needy families containing more than 175 people inside 30 days. This was 25 people more than the prior year. In their initial meeting, Todd, the team's most vocal leader, used this challenge to pull the squad together with two questions: How and how well can WE do it. What you didn't hear was Can we do it?

3. **Individual Responsibility.** The team didn't leave it up to the captains to put the right people in the right roles with the right goals. They all played a hand in determining who would be best suited for specific roles and responsibilities. Coach had a policy that the individual was not spotlighted. He even took it so far as to not give out individual awards, only team awards. The word individual was not allowed to be used unless it was followed by the word responsibility. Coach was right.

They were becoming a team. None of the members needed any outside accountability. They held themselves accountable because they were each invested in the results.

4. **Collective Pride.** Team success is what creates pride, and their collective pride was an outgrowth of service and unselfish acts.

The service and unselfish nature of Morgan Randall, the man, was underscored by the fact that he allowed absolutely no media coverage of this activity. His teams did not do this each year to look good in the eyes of the public. They were motivated to help because service was one of his core values, and the reward was in the very act of serving.

This year, however, the campus public relations people learned about the food drive, and they were all over the story. One of the players must have approached their office for a donation, and that's how they caught wind of it. This was not what Coach had planned and was exactly the kind of thing he despised—shameless self-promotion. Whether it was by an organization, team, or individual, he hated it because it just went against everything he stood for.

Before, Coach had managed to keep the food drive below the radar. This year the public relations office on campus wanted to turn it into a story and release it to the media in the tri-state area. Michael O'Brien, the director of public relations, got no help from Coach. "No. That is not why we do this. We're not doing this to help ourselves; we are doing this to help people who can't help themselves," he argued, frustrated and annoyed.

O'Brien responded by saying, "I'm sending Rodney, our campus photographer, with you whether you like it or not."

Not one to let someone else get the last word in, Randall shot back, "Mike, you tell him he will have to drive himself, and I hope he's psychic. If not, you'd better have enough cameras and enough people to camp out at every church and food pantry in the area because I'm not telling you which one we are going to."

Later that day Coach called the public relations director to apologize and say that he came to his senses. I assumed that the athletic director or university president made him do it. He let O'Brien know that he could meet the team van in front of the administration building the next afternoon, and the photographer could ride along over to the food pantry. He mentioned that the local food pantries were all full, and they had to deliver it to one on the outskirts of town in Coatesville.

Apparently, the operation was so covert that I didn't even have "security clearance" to be briefed on the mission. That afternoon the plan was executed to perfection. Coach had a school van parked in front of the administration building near the public relations director's window. Prior to pulling the van up, the freshmen were assigned the task of loading it with empty boxes and grocery bags to give the appearance of preparing to drop off the Thanksgiving care packages. As they finished loading it, Rodney, the campus photographer, and the public relations director came out of the building and told the freshmen that they would be following the van to the food pantry. Coach pulled up in another vehicle, handed the freshmen directions, and explained that he would meet them there. First he had to pick up some additional frozen turkeys a local grocer was donating at the last minute.

As the decoy vehicle headed due west out of the front gates of campus, the three other vans departed via the back gates on the other end of campus and headed due east to the inner city.

The neighborhood was known as Fairhill and was considered the poorest neighborhood in all of inner city Philadelphia. When we arrived at the shelter and food pantry, Coach received a king's greeting. Men were high-fiving and fist-bumping him, smiling, and asking him about his family and the team's chances at a playoff berth this season. It was clear Coach invested a lot of time over the years doing outreach and helping this under-served community.

The team did an exemplary job distributing the baskets of Thanksgiving dinners to 48 very grateful families. As I handed a mother her family's Thanksgiving basket, she looked up and said, "Coach, my name is Althea Brown, and I just want to thank you. If it weren't for your team doing this, my family was going to have peanut butter and jelly sandwiches on Thanksgiving this year. My father is on hospice right now, and this is probably going to be his last Thanksgiving dinner with us. I can't thank you enough for your generosity."

Seeing the look on Mrs. Brown's face, at that moment I decided that whenever I became a head coach I would carry on this same tradition with my teams.

I loved how it brought the team together in the spirit of giving. It was a total perspective shift. The players gained a greater perspective of how blessed and fortunate they were.

As we traveled back to campus, Randall asked what I thought of the project. "Coach, I think it's great. I'll do the same thing some day with my own team. What Mrs. Brown said was really touching. For what it's worth, while writing my Master's thesis, I learned that research shows there is a direct correlation between organizations with an ethos of making a difference in the community and increased revenue as well as customer and employee retention."

"Jack, that makes perfect sense. I look at our role and the role of the captains as being the keepers of the culture. Our job is to be the change we want to see in the organization."

I agreed, "I'd say today was a big success, but I guess we'll need to wait and see how it translates to teamwork on the field."

"I'm with you there, partner, but I have a feeling my buddy O'Brien and his photographer might not agree. These kinds of activities are like tossing a pebble into a lake. When you throw a pebble into a lake, it creates a ripple effect throughout a large body of water."

"Coach, I'd like to think our example of service to the community might create a ripple effect of inspiring greatness and service throughout the campus."

"Well, at least we won't be reading about it in the newspaper or seeing it on the 6 o'clock news, Jack. Today was a good day. It's always my favorite day of the year. The team worked hard preparing, and the captains did their best, too. Prepare, do your best, then go home and enjoy life. That's what I tell them, and that's my advice to you, Jack. And now I want you to go home and enjoy tonight. Starting tomorrow, you're going to be stuck with me non-stop for the next 3 days. Remember, we leave at 7 A.M.

sharp for the U.S. Lacrosse Coaches Association National Convention up in Connecticut."

Coach understood that in order to gel on the field (in the workplace) his personnel had to first do so off the field (outside the workplace). He understood one fed the other, and the group literally learned how to become a stronger team by feeding others. As a retired Naval officer, Coach understood the value of the concept of service above self. By learning how to serve, you learn the value of leading and leave a legacy. Coach had a team-building blueprint for making a difference and leaving a legacy. It was really as simple as taking three steps: think big, start small, and act now because one person can make a difference. Forty years earlier, the food drive began as one person with a vision, aligning passion and purpose with an ethos of service.

The lesson for me was that you don't need a title to lead. You just need a clear vision and a plan. People will buy in when they feel they work with you, not just for you. Coach was living proof of this. With the help of his team, he was able to use his success and his team's success to create something significant for the community outside the walls of the Radnor University campus. Much of life is really about using your platform to spread good will and serve the community. Do good, and good will follow.

8

SUCCESS OR SIGNIFICANCE

It was an annual tradition in the coaching fraternity—the awards luncheon on day one of the U.S. Lacrosse Coaches Association National Convention. The grand ballroom of the Stamford, Connecticut, Hilton was filled to capacity with at least a thousand coaches, many still hung over from a late night of carousing with friends. Coaches from Division I through junior college were honored for being coach of the year, assistant coach of the year, and reaching certain victory milestones such as the century club for amassing 100 career coaching victories. The 200-, 300-, 400-win club members were honored as well.

As the ceremonies began, I was a little curious, so I asked Coach, "When did you first reach the century club, Coach?"

Randall leaned over and whispered, "Couldn't tell you partner, I don't bother to keep track of that sort of thing. They've got it all wrong. The luncheon is sad for me more than anything else, and I feel sorry for these guys. Our organization is celebrating people who have achieved a certain personal status or fame, not really their values or contributions to the game. Just wins, just a means for them to land their next and higher-paying job. A lot of these guys got what they think they wanted, but their focus is in the wrong place. It's on themselves, not where it ought to be . . . on their student-athletes."

"What do you mean? It seems like a good tradition to honor achievement and longevity."

"Jack, the coaching fraternity generally misunderstands the whole concept of success. We teach young coaches like you to strive for 'success,' you know, to reach a certain status and win trophies, plaques, and awards. Then once they achieve those things like coach of the year, the century club, a big-time Division I coaching job, they'll still be missing the one thing that really matters."

"Which is?" I asked.

"Significance, Jack. It's about significance. Many of their lives are empty. They are striving for success instead of working to know their coaching career meant something to the players who played for them."

"To me success and significance seem like they mean the same thing," I responded.

"A coach of the year award is about what you get. Seeing your players graduate, become husbands and fathers, earn an honest living—that is what you give. Knowing what you taught them played a part in their ability to be the person you knew they could become, now that's significance. Just because these guys are coaches of success doesn't mean they are coaches of significance. These awards, any awards for that matter, are about status, not value."

I could see where the conversation was headed, and it was a real eye-opener for me. I knew he believed there was a huge difference between status and value; it was just the first time I'd seen it. Having the opportunity to attend the awards ceremony, which I had hoped I would be recognized at some day, and then having Coach expose it as a hollow achievement was a total paradigm shift for me. Kind of like the first time you noticed the white arrow between the letter E and the letter X in the FedEx logo. From that day forward every time you see a FedEx ad all you notice is the arrow, not the logo. Today I was seeing something I'd always seen before, but, thanks to Coach, I was looking at it with a new set of eyes.

"What matters is what their players say about them after their playing days are over, maybe after the coach's life is over and their eulogy is being read. What will be said about how you cared about your players and supported them? What sort of legacy did you leave on the coaching profession? Those are the things you need to think about. Forget this awards ceremony. What we do is about the *rewards* of the coaching profession, not the *awards* of the coaching profession."

He wasn't finished yet. "Something else I want you to think about, Jack, is how we got here. The university doesn't budget for professional development for staff members, only for faculty. We can do some recruiting while we're here so our mileage will be paid for, but the actual association dues, this luncheon, and the educational materials we come away from the weekend with, those are all out-of-pocket expenses. I'm going to cover yours because it's important to me to do that for you. I refuse to be like the university. I invest in my people."

"Coach, I didn't know that. You don't have to cover me. I can do that."

"Don't worry, Jack. I can afford it. I'd like to think I'm a little smarter than the folks in human resources. I take training and development seriously. You should write this down so you remember it. I want you to start tithing a percentage of your annual income."

Okay, he'd lost me. I wasn't exactly what you'd call the church-going type, and I thought he knew that.

"I'm not talking about tithing to give to the church, although I do that, too. What I'm talking about is tithing 10 percent of your annual income to put toward your own personal and professional development."

"Why, Coach? Is it really necessary?"

"Like I said before, Jack, write this down. You work on your job, you'll make a living. You work on yourself, you'll make a fortune. There is nothing more important than working on ourselves."

"I never really looked at it that way, Coach. I guess I've just been so wrapped up in working on myself in the academic sense, studying, doing research, writing papers, giving presentations and teaching."

"Jack, I'm not saying that ain't important 'cause it is, but that's all working on your job. We need to have you invest some time working on you. My son Paul is a Methodist minister, and a few years ago I heard one of his sermons on tithing. I really took it to heart. From that day on, I started tithing 30 percent of my income. Ten percent goes to the church, 10 percent to my retirement, and 10 percent to my personal development."

Oh boy, here we were back on the whole church thing again. He was really beginning to lose me.

"Coach, if you hadn't noticed, I'm not the most spiritual guy. Explain this like you're talking to your 6-year-old grandson?"

"Sure thing, Jack. I tithe my time as well as money. So, for example, if you figure out that you have 3 hours of free time a day, try tithing 10 percent of that time and invest it in yourself. Whether it's exercising, writing, or learning a new skill, it's an investment that will pay off down the road."

Given the fact that time was at such a premium for me between grad school and coaching, I immediately fell in love with this idea. Anyone can find 30 minutes in a day. It didn't seem like a lot of time and felt doable.

"Jack, it's a discipline that has a subtle effect. Think of it this way: at the end of the day, a week, a month, the amount of time is hardly noticeable. If you tithe 30 minutes a day over the course of an entire year, that's more than 5 weeks of work."

"Wow, I could actually accomplish a lot in 5 solid weeks."

"Well, I'm glad you see what I mean now, Jack. Imagine what you could do with 3 or even 4 years of tithing 30 minutes a day. The results will be game-changing. So, the same goes for tithing some of your income. If you put aside 10 percent of your paycheck each month, you can use that fund at the end of the year to invest in yourself during the upcoming year."

"You don't need to sell me on the idea, Coach, I'm already sold. But how should I use the money?"

"Well, Warren Buffett, one of my heroes, said the best education he ever got wasn't in college or grad school; it was a public speaking class he took after college that changed his life. That's what I recommend to everyone. Take a public speaking class; invest in some self-help books, seminars, and conferences like this one. Ya' know, it's funny you mentioned my grandson. Little kids are awesome. We should be more like them. You ever see how fascinated they get with the environment around them. Simple stuff I take for granted or flat out overlook and good ole Trey will be spellbound for half an hour over it. That's my goal for you; develop a childlike fascination with working on yourself."

Later that day after a flurry of clinics, seminars, film sessions, and the keynote speech, I sat down in the hotel coffee shop to have a latte while I digested not so much my clinic notes but the bigger issues. The food for thought Coach gave me at the awards luncheon. What would my players say about me after their playing days are over? After my life was over? How would my eulogy read? These were questions I needed to play with. As I finished off my latte, I headed next door to the gift shop. I needed to pick up a journal so I could keep track of these thoughts.

9

THE TWO GREATEST DAYS

On the ride back home from two great days at the coaches convention, the subject of success came back around again. "So, partner, have you thought more about your value as a leader of men? How you ended up in coaching and why? I never did ask you that in the interview."

"Coach, I've been chewing on that ever since lunch. It's not an easy answer."

Coach jumped back in, "You haven't been thinking hard enough then. It will come to you. There were two really great days of my coaching career, and I hope every coach in America has these same two days."

I was curious. Was he kidding? Was this a setup for another one of his signature moments of humor that just sort of sneak up out of a seemingly serious statement to blindside you with a punch line out of left field? The look on his face said maybe not.

"Hey, I'm actually being serious, you maniac! Really, the two best days I've had as a coach were the day I first started coaching as a career and then the day I figured out why I really coach this game."

I knew he was serious because on page three of his team manual, right after his coaching philosophy page, was "Why I Coach." It spelled out exactly what he was about to say.

"It's what successful people do, partner. They figure out what made them successful and why. In my 42 years in this game I've had the privilege of meeting and being mentored by some of the best. I played for Hall of Fame Coach Rich Williams in high school, and on my way up in the profession was exposed to many of his protégés. They all have one thing in common, Jack. They know their purpose."

I nodded and said, "You mean they know why they coach?"

"Sure, but it's more than just coaching. They know why they are here. Why they're put on this planet. Coach Williams explained to me that a man knowing his purpose is like the keel of a ship. It gives you stability. When others around you start abandoning ship when the waters get rough, your purpose (like the keel) will steady the boat to weather the storm."

"I know my first great day was the day you hired me. How do I figure out my why?"

"There are two headings you can take to as you set sail on this journey, Jack. First is to find your passion. What are you truly passionate about? You'll know the answer when you can figure out what you live for and what you'd die for. Passion isn't the be-all, end-all, but it sure will help you set the course toward your true north, your purpose. Passion is the wind behind your sails."

Coach's point was well taken. If you look at great leaders throughout history, they had great energy. Passionate people always do. They love what they're doing because they're doing what they love.

"Jack, your passion is going to be what prevents you from getting destination disease. With passion you learn to love the process more than the destination. Look at me, 42 years later, and I still haven't arrived yet. I don't coach at a big-name school or a lacrosse powerhouse, and I'm good with that, wouldn't want to actually.

And you sure don't see any national championship rings on my fingers, do you?"

"Not yet at least, Coach," I said with a smile.

"Well, Jack, in 42 years that might haunt me just a little, but I don't lose sleep over it. It hasn't discouraged me at all because I still have that wind behind my sails from having an absolute passion for coaching. I don't think you strive to get to the big time; I think the big time is actually a mind-set. In my mind, I've treated everywhere I've coached as already being big time, including little old Radnor."

I was writing furiously in my new journal as I whispered, "Passion." Then I followed up. "So passion is the first heading, gotcha, Coach. What's second?"

"Well, following your passion will get you going in the right direction, but what you need to pair it with is your one thing." All of a sudden, Coach had his signature philosophical look on his face. He got a crease in his brow and his reading glasses dipped down a little lower on his nose so you could see his eyes over them.

"Remember watching that movie City Slickers on the bus ride to our game against Delaware College? Well, there's one scene that stands out. Billy Crystal's character is riding down the trail with Jack Palance's character Curley. Curley looks at him and says 'the secret of life is one thing, just one thing, and that one thing is what you've got to figure out.' Well, Curley was right. We've all got to figure that out."

"Sure I remember that. So I need to figure out my unique talent that sets me apart?"

As usual, Coach's wisdom transcended coaching lacrosse. Everyone has a unique talent or gift they bring to the world; they just have to discover it.

"That's a start, Jack. You can't just figure it out though. You've got to practice it, work it, refine it, and grow it in order to really set yourself apart. I've never met anybody who was successful doing something they didn't love, but equally important you're not gonna be successful doing something you aren't great at. Take a look around campus. You'll see lots of people working there every day who do something they don't love, and they wonder why they struggle or aren't making an impact. They just aren't put in a position to be successful, and that's not all their fault. Somebody put them in that job. Look at Mike in maintenance—great guy, but he wanders around all day with a clipboard in his hand looking busy but not really being productive because he hates what he does. No wonder everything he touches breaks."

"The school systems in the U.S fail our kids because they focus on what's wrong with kids instead of what's right. I remember coming home from high school with a C in math on my report card and an A in history. My teacher told my parents I needed to improve my math skills. I really didn't think that was the answer then, and I still don't think it is now. You want to improve education in this country, put a coach in charge, darn it! Think about it. Look at Jeff on our team. He isn't good at facing off, but he is really good at defense. Why would I have him focus on facing off? He's not fast enough. As a matter of fact, if Jeff got in a race with a pregnant mother, the best he'd finish is third. But he's got a natural talent at defense we can work with and make him great at."

"So, that's Jeff's one thing," I acknowledged.

"Exactly. It's not that he's dumb and can't learn how to face off. It's just that he has a unique gift for playing defense just like I had a unique gift for understanding history not geometry. That's not to say I didn't like geometry; as a matter of fact I liked it so much I took it three times," Coach said with a smirk.

This car ride was sure teaching me about the Xs and Os of success. Coach had a way of making sure sport intersected life and business.

"I remember in 1970 when I was operating my sport fishing business and coaching high school lacrosse in Oyster Bay. I had a conversation that forever changed my life. I was on the dock one morning, and the guy next to me asked me what turned out to be the most important question I'd ever been asked. He said, "Hey, Coach, you've got a nice business going here. I see you're always busy. What's your five-year plan?"

Sport fishing business? I guess I thought he'd been born on a lacrosse field with a whistle around his neck.

"That was Coach version 1.0, as I like to call him. I was just a couple years out of the Navy and didn't really even know I was supposed to have a five-year plan. So, I just decided to BS him and talked about how complex my schedule was and a couple of my goals I had at the time. I was like a cruise ship trying to leave port without raising the anchors, just burning fuel, churning up the water, and going nowhere until I ran out of gas and shut my big fat mouth.

"The fellow just looked at me and said, 'Coach, it's okay. I get it. You don't really have a five-year plan.' That's when he said something that stuck with me and changed the course of my life. He told me a plan doesn't happen automatically. You have to be very strategic about it. 'You're a coach,' he said. 'I've been to your games at the high school. You know all about strategy and game planning. You just need to do it in your own life.'

"That night I went home and told my wife about the conversation I had with this complete stranger. That very same night, she and I started to figure out a five-year plan for me to become a college coach. Four years later we moved out to San Diego, and I got my break as a college coach starting a new lacrosse program at the university there. Twenty-five years and seven new programs later, I'm still planting seeds in this game. Oh, and mama and I still sit down together each year to refine the game plan we have for our own lives."

At that very moment I felt like Coach must have on the dock in 1970. It was becoming clearer and clearer. Successful people don't just have a purpose; they know their purpose and live it intentionally every day. They also make it their mission to add value to the lives of others. Coach mentioned planting seeds, growing the game in new locations, but what he was really doing was way more than that. He was planting seeds of greatness in the minds of all those around him. Helping them grow to their potential.

10

SOCIOLOGY 101

One morning at the crack of dawn, just before fall break, I arrived moments shy of beating Coach to the office. I still hadn't managed to be first. Short of sleeping there, I didn't know how I could. As I rambled in and parked a chair in his cubicle, I blurted out, "Where did you learn how to do this?"

Coach Randall looked a little bewildered, and as usual answered my question with a question. "Learn to do what? Maintain my shapely figure or go undefeated in beating you to the office every morning?" he said with a sly grin.

"The latter, but now that you mention it, your comment is a perfect example of something else I want to talk to you about, Coach. You always have the right words at the right time. Where did you learn how to do that?"

Coach leaned in closely and whispered, "My wife bought me one of those videotape instructional courses on the Home Shopping Network on TV. Wanna borrow it?"

Not knowing whether he was kidding or serious, I paused and hoped for a response indicating an answer one way or the other. You never knew with Coach. It was part of his charm, I guess. Then after what felt like an eternity, he burst out with a belly laugh and said, "Lighten up, would ya'? I'm just having a little fun with you. Or are you still pouting that I beat you in here again?"

Leaning his chair back, Coach explained his philosophy on communication. "I'm gonna sum up my answer to your question in one four-letter word, okay?"

Fearing what might fly out of Coach's mouth next, I simply nodded in agreement.

"Bass is the word. GOT it, partner?" Coach said.

"You mean like the freshwater fish?" I asked.

"No, you maniac. Like the acronym! BASS. It's one of those mnemonic devices teachers teach students to use when studying. Which, by the way, I really think was just invented to help old people remember complicated stuff.

"BASS stands for Be A Social Scientist. There, my friend. Now you have the keys to the kingdom."

Wanting at least something resembling an explanation, I asked for more.

"If you get in the habit of always being a social scientist, you'll learn to be more present in the moment and connect better with people by being locked in to what is going on around you. Too many people live with their faces buried in their cell phones and computer screens."

"Okay, but what's that have to do with why I can never seem to beat you to the office?"

"Don't worry. Nobody ever does, partner. I get here first for one reason, BASS. Take a look. I've got my desk facing the window for a reason. I like to see, not just when, but also how people show up here. Do they come racing in and storm out of their car in a hurry? Are they smiling when they walk up to the door? Who are they walking with or talking to?"

Seeing confusion on my face, he continued. "You see, Jack, I'll be the first to tell you I keep my eyes open and take whatever lessons or strategies I can from folks around me. You can do the same thing. Whether it's another lacrosse coach, the baseball coach, an NFL football coach, a local businessman in our booster club, or one of my sons.

"If I see something I like, something I can use to help my team, I'll try to make it work. I'll tweak it and make it my own because I can't be a carbon copy of one of those guys. I have to be myself because in the end I'm the only person I know well enough to really count on. Be a social scientist, but most importantly be yourself."

"Well now, I guess I'm totally confused. On the bus last week, you told me to put away that Vince Lombardi book I was reading. And now you're telling me to learn new strategies from other coaches and business people?"

"Jack, the other day on the bus my exact words were 'Don't try to be the next Vince Lombardi, just be the best Jack Burton.' And I still mean that. He's an icon, but trust me, Lombardi's a bad example to emulate. The things he did to professional athletes a couple generations ago won't work on today's generation of amateur athletes we coach."

Coach had touched on something very important that happens to people in every line of work: bias. Everybody has a philosophy, and they're biased toward it because they either saw it work for someone else or it worked for them to a certain extent.

It's a double-edged sword, though, because when you experience losses or adversity, self-doubt about your philosophy can creep in. Goals that are unmet threaten your core values. You have to be willing to grow and change, but not compromise the core values that guide you. That's the benefit of an outside perspective.

"Here is how we are going to get you equipped, partner. There are three lessons I want you to learn, and because fall break is coming up, now is the perfect time for you to learn and start practicing them."

"I have five sons; they're all champions in their own right. You haven't met them yet, but you will someday. I've learned as much from them as they ever learned from me, and I want you to have the same benefit.

"So here is how we're gonna do it. Three of them work in fields that relate directly to what we do, and I want you to learn from them. I wish I could afford to send you to interview them, but since this is Division III, we don't exactly have a booster on speed dial to loan us his Learjet. So, we've got to use local folks in the same jobs who are willing to help."

"Really? You mean to tell me you don't have a private pilot on speed dial? I mean, after all, you're the same guy who's got his own customized golf cart."

"What can I tell you, kid? At my age you learn not to go to the well too often for stuff," Coach said with a smirk.

"Here's the plan, Jack. My youngest son, Tim, is a United States Marine. What I know about discipline and recruiting I learned from him. I want you to go to the recruiting station across town and interview the Colonel down there. Call the office today, ask for Colonel Roger Duncan, and remind him I sent you. He's got Tuesday open for you on his schedule."

"Okay, Coach, let me write all this down."

"Please. That's another habit you need to get into, Jack.

"Next is my son Paul. He's the Methodist minister I told you about. Everything I know about communicating with passion and influence and having faith I learned from him. I want you to go visit the pastor at my local church and interview him. I've already set this one up, too; he's expecting you at his place Wednesday morning."

"A preacher? Okay, I just hope he doesn't mind that I haven't been to church in years."

"Don't worry, Jack. Pastor Rich is one of the greatest and most accepting men you will ever meet. Besides, I warned him about you," Coach said, once again with his patented smirk.

"My oldest son, Morgan, Jr., is one of the top media sales executives in New York City. I've learned a lot about relationship building and persistence from him. I want you to meet with J.J. Andrews on Monday. He's a media executive over at the local radio station. You'd never know it from talking to him, but J.J.'s one of the biggest celebrities in this area. You've probably either heard of him or heard him on the radio. If you can learn how to sell something invisible like air, then selling a family on a college education ought to be easy."

"Great point, Coach. I never thought of it that way, but yes. We aren't selling something tangible either; it's more of an experience."

"Jack, use the break next week to meet with these folks and work on yourself. Take great notes, and you can report back to me on this when the semester starts up again Monday a week. Okay, partner?"

As I walked out of Coach's office, I started thinking about that fateful day I met Ben out on the lacrosse field in Burlington. What he said was right on the money. This really was beginning to feel like the equivalent of an MBA candidate interning with Warren Buffett. I never imagined my calendar next week would look like it did.

11

THE INVISIBLE

Bright and early Monday morning I began my trek up the stairs of the radio station's corporate office, armed "coach style" with a pen and yellow legal pad. The executive I was scheduled to meet, J.J. Andrews, was one of the tri-state area's most successful young entrepreneurs. He owned eight radio stations, an entertainment magazine, a racetrack, and the Front Porch Café, a popular coffee shop right around the corner from campus. All of which landed him on the "Top 40 under 40" list of Pennsylvania's most successful executives.

Before I could open the glass double doors at the entrance, a young man in a navy Giorgio Armani pinstripe suit and scarlet Brioni power tie bounded out to greet me. "Welcome to Majestic Media Group. I'm J.J. and you must be Jack. Any friend of the Coach is a friend of mine.

"He wanted me to talk to you a little bit about sales and communication. You probably couldn't have come to a better place for that considering we're in the broadcast communications business.

"So, then let's start at the beginning of everything. Nothing, and I mean NOTHING, happens until something gets sold. I said we're in the broadcasting business, but really we're in the sales business first.

"Our job is really to get listeners to see the invisible. Radio is all about theater of the mind, Jack. If you want to make a compelling call to action with an ad, you've got to paint a picture for the listener. It's the same with recruiting student-athletes or selling anyone anything for that matter. You've got to paint a picture for them and give them a compelling reason to respond to you.

"Here's the secret. My best salespeople don't just paint a picture for the client; they also paint the client into the picture. You can do the same thing recruiting; you're selling the invisible every bit as much as we are when you make that first phone call. Education is an abstract thing; you can't pull a box of it off the shelf and hand it to someone.

"Let's move this conversation from the office to the studio. I do a daily sports talk show, and I'd like you to sit in live on-air with me. I can teach you more in an hour on the air than a week sitting around talking. We can talk in the car and break everything down during the commercial breaks."

As J.J. led the way out to the parking lot, I wondered where on earth he was going and stopped to ask. He explained the studio was not located at the corporate office like most radio stations. "We take our show on the road and broadcast live from the Big Apple from 5 to 7 P.M. every night."

"The Big Apple as in New York?" I asked, a bit perplexed.

"Ha ha, I'm sorry, no, not the city. The Big Apple is a sports bar in town. We take our show on the road to where our listeners are."

A year earlier J.J. had the idea to take the invisible and make it visible by partnering with the most popular nightspot in town, building a radio studio inside the sports bar, and broadcasting there live each night.

A bold move, no doubt, I thought. But, I asked, "Has it been successful?"

"We went from the doghouse to the penthouse in the ratings inside of six months. For the first time ever, people could see, touch, feel, listen, and interact with a radio station live and in person. Meanwhile the competition still remains invisible; you've got to tune in to hear them."

"Very cool concept. I love how interactive you made it."

"Jack, before you sit down behind the mike, I want you to flip the switch. What I mean by that is you are a person off the air, and on the air you are a personality, larger than life. You've got to play the role to make the connection. So when you walk in the studio doorway, flip the switch and be that personality.

"It's the same thing when you're recruiting; you've got to flip the switch before you walk into the meeting or the prospect's living room. It's show time! People want to be entertained as much if not more than they want to be informed. You've got to be what I call an info-tainer; inform them but entertain at the same time. It will make your message memorable while your competitors will all sound and look the same. Why do you think Coach has such a larger-than-life personality? Because he flips the switch."

I grinned, responding, "Yeah, but I think sometimes he forgets to unflip it."

The hour on-air felt like 5 minutes as we discussed the Philadelphia Eagles' quarterback woes, the Phillies off-season trades, and everything in between. As we removed our headphones, turned off the mikes, and unflipped the switch, J.J. looked at me with a wry smile and asked, "Was it fun?"

I tried to contain myself but was so pumped I just shouted out, "It felt like game day. The last time I was this amped up I was playing lacrosse in college." With that J.J. pointed around the studio and said in a very matter-of-fact tone, "None of this would have happened if management here wasn't sold.

"Sales is the most important job in the world, Jack; and if you ask me, it's the best job in the world. I'm not exaggerating when I tell you it's the best job I've ever had. Tons of perks, freedom, and great relationships, and the pay is out of this world, too. In what other job can you have the opportunity to give yourself a raise every day?" J.J. queried rhetorically.

"Why did you stop doing it?"

"Why did I stop doing it? I'm not sure I ever really did, Jack. No one ever does. You just incorporate those skills into your climb up the corporate ladder. Whether your goal is to be a head coach, CEO, entrepreneur, a doctor, or anything else, the ability to sell and persuade is the most important skill set you can develop."

J.J. was definitely on a roll. So I asked him how sales skills could help people in other jobs.

He was ready for my question. "The art of selling teaches you how to schmooze, pitch, and negotiate. More importantly, you'll learn how to sell your projects and ideas. Most importantly, you learn how to sell yourself. Which, I might add, you're gonna need big time in recruiting.

"Take this to the bank, Jack. You learn how to sell and it won't just improve your career, it'll improve your life. There is no doubt it will make it easier for you to do all kinds of stuff you have to do in life. Stuff like buying and selling things, getting help from difficult people, even dealing with insurance companies. Then when you're a little older like me, it will help you in negotiating with your wife and kids.

"Going into sales was one of the best decisions I've made in my life. That's why I think every CEO, entrepreneur, teacher, coach, and manager should spend some time in formal sales. The earlier the better, I might add."

Whether it was his sheer enthusiasm or a light coming on in my own brain, J.J.'s words had me wondering about how I might apply sales in my coaching. "Thanks, J.J. What are some fundamentals I can apply to coaching?"

As we made our way out of the Big Apple back to J.J.'s silver Jaguar XJS sedan, he gave me a friendly pat on the back, smiled, and said, "Sure, let's talk in the car on the way."

During the commute, J.J. shared what he called his fistful of sales or five fundamentals of selling.

"I'm going to give you five techniques, one for each finger on your hand. Use these techniques individually, and you can slap prospects around so to speak. Use them together, and they make a fist. Which is more powerful, a slap or a punch?"

Giving him my best "I get it" nod, I prepared myself for the first in my week-long learning sessions.

J.J. rolled up his shirtsleeves as we approached a red light.

"Okay, here's your first technique," J.J. said as he raised up his index finger. "It's called 'Shut up'! You have two ears and one mouth for a good reason. There is nothing you have to say about your product or company that is nearly as important as what the prospect has to say to you. There is a danger in saying too much when selling. Answer their question, shut up, and listen. What they tell you are clues. They will tell you how to sell them if you just shut up and listen."

My first thought was that this advice seemed to explain a lot about Coach Randall. "I sometimes tease Coach that he's a man of few words around some people. He answers questions matter-of-factly with short statements and then just listens. It kind of reminds me of Obi-Wan Kenobi in *Star Wars*. Now I know why he does it."

"That's right, Jack. He does it because it works.

"Number two is that adversity creates advantage. These are in rank order by the way, Jack, so keep that in mind. The most important opportunity to make a difference is always when something has gone wrong."

Time to show I was, indeed, paying attention. I spoke up. "I get it, J.J.—kind of like the situation with the competition when you created the Big Apple studio concept."

"Good catch, Jack. That's right. If the competition wasn't eating our lunch in the ratings, I may not have felt compelled to make what was, looking back, a pretty bold move. So, for example, how you respond to adversity when a customer or prospect pushes back on something is a window into your potential. That adversity will bring with it an equal element of advantage, if you have the courage to step up to the plate and deliver.

"Number three is that the buyer or customer is king. But your customer isn't just the prospect you're trying to sign. You've got a lot more customers than that. In my business, the advertiser and the listener are my obvious customers. We call them external customers. Then there's another whole set of customers back at the office—my employees, co-workers, and colleagues inside the company. They're my internal customers.

"You've got them back at the university as well. You don't sign that blue-chip recruit unless the groundskeeper makes one heck of a great first impression with the physical appearance of the campus when the recruit and his parents pull onto campus. Then that second impression is made by the custodian when the kid and his family walk in your building. Treat those folks like royalty. Their seemingly insignificant jobs are the most significant of all. Either of those experiences goes bad, and you've got no shot at the kid."

"Got it, J.J.," I blurted out while I furiously scribbled notes onto my pad.

As we approached the intersection, J.J. raised his hand out the car's sunroof and stuck up four fingers. "Put these fingers together, and we've almost got a fist, Jack. The fourth thing to understand is that I am not in the radio business, you are not in the coaching business, the lawyer in that corner office is not in the legal business; we are ALL in the relationship business.

"A lot of people make big corporations out to be evil, corrupt, money-grubbing enterprises. That couldn't be further from the truth. These big corporations, just like teams, are run by people. The successful ones realize that doing business is all about relationships. Look at Walmart, General Electric, and IBM. They were numbers four, six, and seven in the Fortune 500 for revenue this year. At the foundational level, their success is simply because their people work together to reach a set of shared goals.

"Research shows that grades improve when students have relationships with their professors, and employees are more engaged at work when they know their manager cares about them. Be in the relationship business first, then the coaching business, Jack."

As we approached Majestic Media's headquarters, J.J. shared his fifth and final technique with me.

"This last one is probably the toughest, Jack. You've got to empathize with and appeal to your decision maker's motives. Whether it's one of my account executives trying to sell a *Monday Night Football* sponsorship or you trying to sign a high school All-American or anything else for that matter, there's going to be a decision maker. In your case, it isn't always the prospect. Sometimes it's mom or dad.

"Once you've identified who that decision maker is and you understand what their motives are, in other words their WIIFM, or *what's in it for me*, then you can start to appeal to them effectively. Not a minute sooner."

I started to put the cap on my pen and throw my legal pad back into my Nike messenger bag. "Okay, J.J., I think I've got the fist: shut up, adversity creates advantage, buyer is king, relationship business, and empathize with the decision maker's motives."

"You got it nailed! An easy way to remember this is the acronym SABRE. Oh, and one more thing, Jack. Selling and coaching are both tough gigs because everything happens in real time. There's no room for Monday morning quarterbacking. An advantage is that you get to learn under fire. You'll see very quickly that what's cool about this is that it naturally accelerates the learning process. There is absolutely no better way to learn business skills. Let me know how I can help you sell yourself and sell Radnor. And, by the way, I look forward to seeing you on game day."

As I drove home from my meeting, I had a lot to think about, but strangely my mind kept coming back to one thing: the concept of imagination. J.J. and Coach each had vivid and wonderful imaginations. It was a job requirement given the work Coach had done in his career, starting seven collegiate programs from scratch. How do you take something from concept to reality, grow it, and nurture it without imagination and vision?

Imagination is especially critical in the small college coaching environment. You have to be a solutions-oriented thinker to survive, much less thrive, when dealing with challenges like budget cuts, limited staffing, lack of facilities, and personnel issues like youth and lack of depth.

It seemed that Coach recruited imagination in a prospect as much as talent and intelligence. He must have because that would explain why there was such great team chemistry on the squad. Most of the players were big dreamers themselves. With a new program they had to imagine what their future could be at Radnor, have trust, keep the faith, and then work hard every day to achieve that vision.

12

SEMPER FI

As I headed for the local Marine Corps recruiting station on Tuesday to meet Colonel Duncan, my thoughts wandered from being a social scientist to thinking about my dad's service in the Air Force. My father, Lt. Colonel Franklin Burton, was a highly decorated World War II fighter pilot, and our family held military service in the highest regard. I knew there were some common elements to military service in each branch, but I also knew the United States Marine Corps was unique. So I couldn't wait to meet the Colonel.

As I walked in the office, I was greeted by a behemoth of a man, a highly decorated officer in the standard delta blue dress uniform. I could tell he was an officer because his trousers had the 2-inch-wide scarlet blood stripe down the outer seams, which was unique to the Marine Corps. "Good morning, sir. I'm Jack Burton. Are you Colonel Duncan?"

"Yes, welcome and good morning, Jack. Let's take a walk around the facility while we talk. I'll show you around," he said. "By the way, did Coach happen to tell you how I came into this job?"

Not knowing where he was going with the question, I simply replied, "No, he just told me to meet with you."

The Colonel explained, "The Marine Corps is the only branch of the service that holds recruiting as the highest honor bestowed upon an officer. Imagine if every organization operated as we do and held the recruiter as the highest possible position. It's part of the legacy you get to leave before you retire from the Corps. You have the opportunity to shape the future of the organization."

I was already impressed and not shy to voice my admiration. "To serve in that role sounds like a great honor, Colonel, and an even greater responsibility."

"My job's not that different than yours, Jack. We get assigned to recruiting stations, substations, and officer selection stations all over the country. As recruiters, it's our job to visit high schools, sit down kneecap-to-kneecap and talk with families, and answer questions to help high school students better understand and prepare for service in the Corps. You and I both have to have the ability to convince complete strangers to dedicate their lives to our organization for at least four years. That takes a special kind of person."

I could already see why Coach had chosen this man to talk to me.

"I agree, Colonel. Recruiting's the life's blood of organizations. Coach and I view it as the most important job at the university. Without recruiting, the doors would close permanently."

Colonel Duncan picked up his pace as we walked. "You're right, Jack, but unfortunately I'm afraid most folks in corporate America don't see it that way. Recruiters at most companies play it safe. They cast a wide net and then hire the person with the best recommendations or whoever looks the best on paper. What they neglect to realize is the game's not played on paper.

"Look at the people who came with wonderful recommendations. Did you really expect them to list people on their résumé who would give them a poor recommendation? And the people who look great on paper. How do they respond to adversity? To getting knocked down?

"Those intangibles, that's what we measure. We look for quality, not quantity. Constantly searching for that diamond in the rough—that's how we recruit, and I know Coach Randall does the same."

I could see he knew Coach well. "Yeah, he talks a lot about intangibles as opposed to 40-yard dash times, height, weight, and strength. He likes to say that not everything that matters can be measured and not everything that can be measured matters. I told him that was a quote from Albert Einstein, but he insists he came up with it first and Einstein stole it from him."

The Colonel laughed. "Coach is a character for sure, but he's right about one thing. Your game isn't played on paper either, so as a college recruiter you darn well ought to do the same thing we do. The most important resource we have isn't artillery or ammunition or even technology. It's the human resource. Same with you.

"You're only as good as the people you surround yourself with. They need to have strong work ethic, intelligence, and loyalty. If they have the first two but not the last one, they will destroy your team faster than you could ever build it."

"How do you keep your standards so high, Colonel?"

"Personally, I treat all my applicants as if they were already Marines. I teach them our core values and the standards we live by and again, quality over quantity. I make sure we're not just letting anyone join.

"The other thing I do is ask my recruiters these two questions: Can you see yourself leading this individual in the future? Is he or she someone you'd want as your lance corporal? If they even so much as hesitate in answering, I know we need to keep searching. They just found hay, not the needle in the haystack.

"You could do the same thing with your upperclassmen. Ask them if they would want a particular recruit to be their teammate next year or if they could see that freshman stepping in and contributing when it matters most."

Ah ha. Now he was talking my language. "That's a great strategy, Colonel. I'll do it. Our recruiting process starts by evaluating high school sophomores and juniors, then they commit and sign as seniors. How does your process work?"

"I think most people would be surprised to find out just how extensive the recruiting process is. There's a misconception that if someone walks in my office and wants to be a Marine, we just have them sign papers, hand them a camouflage uniform, and ship them off to Parris Island for basic training.

"When folks find out everything we do, they're surprised. Have you thought about how you're going to assess your candidates' work ethic, intelligence, and loyalty?"

"No, but I suspect I'd like to model what I'm doing after your process. It's probably why Coach sent me here."

The officer's gunmetal blue eyes lit up when he heard this. "The Marine Corps was built on sound moral values and leadership characteristics; great teams are, too. Marines rely on each other every day, so as a result we have to teach, drill, test, and expect the highest level of character from each and every member of our team. And that includes our leaders, too. Same holds true for your program.

"Have you thought about what your core values are, Jack? Our core values are honor, courage, and commitment. I had to memorize this in boot camp, and I'll never forget it. You should create core values for your team, too."

By now, the fingers of my writing hand were nearing numbness, but I scribbled furiously. "How do you define your core values, Colonel?"

"Honor means a Marine will live by the highest ethical and moral standards, have respect for others, and act in a responsible, mature, and dependable manner. Without honor, the other two values lack real meaning," he explained.

"Courage means a Marine has the ability to face fear and overcome it. We will use mental, moral, and physical strength to steady ourselves in times of stress, rise to the challenge, and face the new and the unknown. What helped me get through Parris Island was knowing that mental toughness was as important as physical toughness. I'd like to think I'm pretty mentally tough.

"Commitment is our final core value. It means Marines feel determined and dedicated to a purpose. We vow to serve something bigger than ourselves and won't stop until a goal is reached," he concluded.

The Colonel maneuvered his way over to the navy blue wall behind his mahogany desk. "Take a look on the wall over here, Jack. These are our leadership traits."

You could tell that the words were hand painted with precision in a very official looking red and white block font. The list of 14 traits looked remarkably familiar to the locker room wall back at Radnor.

Our Leadership Traits dictate that all members of Marine leadership will demonstrate:

- Justice, giving consideration to each side of a situation and assigning rewards or punishment based on merit

- Judgment, weighing facts and possible solutions on which to base sound decisions

- Dependability, performing duties properly, on time and to the best of their abilities

- Initiative, taking action in the absence of orders to solve a problem

- Decisiveness, making decisions quickly and executing them effectively

- Tact, acting politely and avoiding offense while dealing with others

- Integrity, acting truthfully and honestly, showing good character and soundness of moral principles

- Enthusiasm, showing sincere interest and excitement in the performance of an activity

- Bearing, creating a favorable impression in appearance and personal conduct at all times

- Unselfishness, acting considerately and avoiding personal advancement at the expense of others

- Courage, acting calmly and confidently in the face of fear, danger or criticism

- Knowledge, having a wide range of information, including professional knowledge and an understanding of team members' capabilities

- Loyalty, showing faithfulness to country, family, friends, subordinates and peers

- Endurance, having the mental and physical stamina to withstand pain, fatigue, stress and hardship

The Colonel smiled as he watched me finish reading the list. "Have any questions, Jack?"

"Well, after looking at the 14 traits on the wall, I know where Coach got the idea for the 18 Spartan Traits & Citizen Values listed on our locker room wall. But we're having a heck of a time getting the guys to memorize them. How do you get your men to remember them?"

Colonel Duncan eased back in his burgundy leather desk chair and speaking in almost a whisper said, "I think I can help you with that. It's going to be extremely important that your players understand the meaning of each leadership trait and how to develop it so they know what goals to set as they work to be good leaders and good followers.

"The 14 leadership traits are foundational qualities of thought and action that, when demonstrated in a Marine's daily activities,

help him or her earn the respect, confidence, and loyal coopera-
tion of fellow Marines. It's why it's so important for a Marine to
always be able to remember the basic leadership traits.

"We use the acronym J.J. DID TIE BUCKLE to make it easy to
remember. Each letter in the acronym corresponds to the first letter of one of the traits. By remembering the acronym, you will be
better able to recall the traits. Create an acronym for your Spartan
traits."

I could see I had some work ahead. As I jotted down J.J. DID TIE
BUCKLE on my legal pad, I could see the Colonel reaching into
his desk drawer for something.

"Colonel, I have one other question if that's okay. What's your
biggest challenge as a leader?"

"Your timing is impeccable, Jack. Have you ever heard the term
Ductos Exemplo?"

"No, sir, I haven't, and my Latin is a little rusty."

"It means to lead by example. The biggest challenge is leadership by example, plain and simple. As a recruiter I've got to go out
and sell people every day on the fact that we are the most elite
fighting force in the world. If this is really true and we are the
nation's best, well then, I need to demonstrate that 110 percent of
the time myself."

I immediately thought of Vince Lombardi's quote emblazoned on
our team handbook and shared it with the Colonel. "Winning is
not a some of the time thing, it's an all of the time thing. You
don't win once in a while, you don't do things right once in a
while; you do them right all the time. Winning is a habit."

"Jack, Coach and I both love that quote. Here is a card I keep in a number of places. On it you'll find our leadership principles, the principles that dictate what we as leaders are charged with doing."

As he passed a credit-card-sized, gold-laminated card across the desk to me, I could see the words *Ductos Exemplo* across its front and on the back 11 leadership principles. After I glanced at the card, I looked up with a smile and said, "They don't make you memorize this, too, do they, Colonel?"

Duncan let out a belly laugh and explained that indeed they do, but it isn't enough to simply have something as important as the principles in the back of your mind ready for recall. They need to be top of mind.

"I memorized the 11 principles when I became an officer, and *Ductos Exemplo* is the motto of Officer Candidate School. But what I learned was the longer I led my unit, the more I realized I needed to know them and commit to them on a deeper level. Let me put it to you this way, Jack. Why does Coca-Cola advertise?"

I was wondering if this was a trick question but took a chance and answered anyway. "Because they want more business?"

"You're on the right track. They advertise because it works. When you're thirsty, you're more inclined to reach for a Coke because they've made thousands of brand impressions in your mind. No one ever said to themselves, 'I'm dying for an ice-cold glass of Sam's Club Cola.' So, by keeping the 11 principles on a card in my wallet, on my desk, at my nightstand, on my screen saver, and in my car, I'm advertising to myself that I need to lead by example in all 11 areas all the time."

I took a deeper look at the principles on the card.

Our Leadership Principles dictate that leaders of Marines will:

- Be technically and tactically proficient

- Know themselves and seek self-improvement

- Know their Marines and look out for their welfare

- Keep their Marines informed

- Set the example

- Ensure the task is understood, supervised, and accomplished

- Train their Marines as a team

- Make sound and timely decisions

- Develop a sense of responsibility in their subordinates

- Employ their unit in accordance with its capabilities

- Seek responsibility and take responsibility for their actions

Colonel Duncan added, "In keeping with the theme of Coke's advertising, beyond all the commercials, jingles, ads, and mass marketing, it has a slogan, too, doesn't it?"

"It's 'Always Coca-Cola.' But what's that have to do with the Marine Corps?"

Colonel Duncan handed me what appeared to be a small gold hatpin. "What does that say underneath the logo?" he asked.

"It says Semper Fidelis, sir, which if my memory of Latin serves me correctly means Always Faithful."

"That's right, Jack, your Latin's not so rusty after all. That's our slogan, and it dates back to 1883. A lot of people know what Semper Fidelis means, but they don't know what it means to a Marine. It's not just something we carry on a pin or emblem. It symbolizes the trust and morale we carry inside us. It means watching out for your brothers to your left and to your right, watching their backs at work and off-duty, too.

"It's not something that's given to you. It's something you develop throughout your Marine Corps career. I think Coach brought you here because that is the same sense of legacy, esprit de corps, pride, and tradition he wants to cultivate in his teams year in and year out. Now, like me here at the Corps, you're a part of the leadership at Radnor. It's your responsibility to impress upon the young men you lead this one fact. When they join the team at Radnor, they're picking up the torch and putting on the uniform of the players who came before them and laid the groundwork with blood, sweat, and tears to get the program where it is."

I could see what the Colonel meant now; Semper Fidelis is way more than a slogan or motto. It's about a Marine always being faithful to our country and to the Corps. This was something Coach and I wanted with our players, to get them to be more faithful to the team and the campus community. My visit to the recruiting station reinforced the fact that we needed to advertise that better to the team.

"I do have another question, Colonel. I know we've got an all-volunteer military here in the United States and serving as a college-athlete is a privilege and voluntary activity as well. For you, what's the greatest reward of military service?"

"Great question. But before I answer, can you tell me why you're asking?" he countered.

"I ask because I want to be able to sell the rewards of committing and putting in that dedicated Spartan effort to our guys."

"Well, I'll tell you, Jack, one of the greatest rewards about serving in the Marines is that there's no such thing as an ex-Marine or a former Marine. Once a Marine, always a Marine. Becoming a Marine is a transformation that cannot be undone, and Semper Fidelis is a permanent reminder of that."

His comments made me reflect on my own experience as a college athlete. My coaches always treated me the same way Marines treat one another; like a member of the team even after I graduated. Our mascot was the Devil, and it really was a once a Devil, always a Devil mind-set. My teammates and I still follow the program; we still support it and keep coming back to campus as proud alums.

This meeting was a great reminder that you have to be loyal to something. You can't just be loyal in and of itself. For Duncan, you have to be loyal to the Corps and to your fellow Marines. And that relates to our team as well. You will always be a member of the program even after graduation.

I began to realize that Semper Fidelis distinguishes the Marine Corps bond from any other. It goes beyond teamwork—it's a brotherhood that can always be counted on. I wanted to create that same bond with the Radnor players and then ultimately with my own teams when I became a head coach.

Colonel Duncan pointed toward the recruiting station lobby as he said, "Jack, I think our jobs are more similar than you realize. See that family over there with my Master Sergeant? Their son is enlisting today, and for most parents, it's something that is foreign and frightening.

"Sending a young adult they've raised off to college is probably very similar for most parents. It's the culmination of everything they've done as parents. Then they turn them over to us, and we take it a step further. They raise them from a child to a man, and we take them and help them become better men.

"In our own ways, we take them to a level they didn't know they had. We take them to a place where they can; in the Marine Corps there is no 'I can't.' When we get done with a recruit, in that soldier's mind nothing is impossible. You do the same thing. We do it on the battlefield, and you do it on the athletic field."

By now, I was nodding in full agreement. "That's probably the best thing about coaching, Colonel. You go out and work with players on developing a certain skill to help their game. They don't know how to do it initially, but you keep working with them, coaching and encouraging them, and having them practice every day. Then one day, maybe weeks or months down the road, they execute that skill to perfection in a game. The look in their eye is priceless, and the best part is that they then feel that if they can do that, they can accomplish anything."

Now it was the Colonel's turn to smile in agreement. "Now you know why I do what I do, Jack. I think you've got a promising career ahead of you. Let me know how I can help. I'll see you at the season opener. I haven't missed one since I got stationed here!"

13

FAITH

After meetings with two people who seemed larger than life, I had the feeling my Wednesday visit would bring a different experience. Today I was visiting Pastor Rich, who had asked me to meet him at his lake house for coffee.

When I got there, he was friendliness itself. "Morning, Jack. Door's always open, come on in. I've got a cup of coffee here for you."

But we didn't stay inside long. As soon as I got my coffee, he said, "It's a nice day. Why don't we go for a walk? It's part of my daily ritual with my dog, Beau, to take a walk of gratitude around the lake. I'm grateful for visiting with you today, and you'll see rather quickly that my wacky ol' retriever is grateful for, well, darn near every tree on the property."

Laughing aloud, I knew I was in for an enjoyable visit.

"When Coach told me he wanted us to meet, I did a little thinking and decided that I've got four pieces of wisdom to share with you that I learned over the years from my mentor, Reverend Scott Peters.

"Before we head out, let me ask you this. I've got two magazines on the coffee table in front of you; look at the covers and tell me which one you'd rather read."

I glanced down at the two publications on the mahogany table, *Time* magazine and *Sports Illustrated*. The cover of *Time* was adorned with a picture of a slightly overweight, balding, middle-aged man wearing a suit and Coke-bottle glasses. The headline read, "How Alan Greenspan views the economy." The *Sports Illustrated* happened to be its swimsuit edition. On the cover was a photo of supermodel Tyra Banks in a skimpy, red polka-dot two-piece with a headline that read "NOTHiNG BUT BiKiNiS."

I knew my choice right away but was feeling a little uncomfortable telling the pastor that I would opt for the swimsuit edition. Fortunately my worries were cast aside when Rich interjected, "I'm no gambler, but I'd bet the mortgage on the parsonage that you'd choose *Sports Illustrated*. Tell the truth, Jack. Am I right or what?"

I bashfully replied, "I have to admit, yes, you figured me out."

"It's okay, Coach. I don't have any problem with that. I know why you chose that, and the reason is quite simple. *Sports Illustrated* is more entertaining than *Time* magazine, especially the swimsuit edition, and people would rather be entertained than informed," Rich said with a sly grin.

As he refilled both our coffee cups with fresh java, he continued, "Once you understand this concept of human nature, you can best alter your message and its delivery to meet the needs of your audience. I deal with the same issue with my congregation. People could sooner tell you the lyrics to the new Bon Jovi song than recite Philippians 4:8.

"They don't want to hear another boring sermon; they want me to be entertaining, funny, witty, and energetic. As a matter of fact, they expect that and demand that of me. I've been doing this long enough to know that if I don't entertain them in this week's service, there's a good chance I won't see them next week.

"Your audience wants that from you, too, Jack. If you're not interesting and entertaining, they won't opt to attend Radnor. That was lesson number one. I'll share two others with you while we walk."

As we set out on our walk around Lake Norman, I noticed that Rich's pace was brisk for a man of his years. "Jack, the best way to entertain and inform people at the same time is by telling them a story. Start with a story, grab their attention immediately with your strongest point or part of your message and then you can weave the educational points throughout the story. I call it info-tainment. My best friend Dr. Ding, a professor over at Radnor, calls it edutainment. Do you know him?"

"No, Rich, I haven't met him yet. Guess I'd better schedule a meeting because he sounds like an interesting guy. So how does this concept of info-tainment relate to recruiting?"

"What you want to do, Jack, is tell a story, relate your prospect's experience they would have to a past experience a current player or former player has had. Obviously, I use parables from the Bible to illustrate my points. You can do something similar with stories from your team or past teams. However, I've seen your schedule. If you wanted to use the story of David and Goliath as an analogy, that wouldn't be a bad choice either."

"Thanks for reminding me, Pastor. Maybe you could tell Coach to lighten up the schedule a bit for next year."

We both laughed for a moment or two, but Pastor Rich was all business and got us right back on point. "You see, the way story-telling works is when you use an example of a family's experience with your program when speaking with a group of parents, every parent in the room will be thinking not of that child's experience but of their child potentially having a similar experience. Think of it as a strategy to turn listening into engagement and 'them' into 'us.'"

I could immediately see the sense of what Rich was saying. "I guess it's why testimonials and success stories are such effective selling tools."

"Exactly, Jack. You just want to be sure to avoid what I call 'sky-scraper sermons,' or in your case the skyscraper sales pitch. That would be what I call piling one story on top of another to the point where you bore your audience to tears. Use one good story to reinforce your point. Then stop."

As we reached the halfway point around the lake, Rich stopped at a well-aged wooden bench, and we sat down to admire a field of the brightest, most brilliant flowers I had ever seen. "Rich, I know this is your property, but did you . . .?"

Rich cut me off before I could finish my question. "Yes, I planted every single one of them myself. It's a tribute to my wife, Peg. I started it after the cancer took her leg, and then I finished it, all 25,000 bulbs, after it took the rest of her four years ago this month."

Speechless for a moment, I finally stammered, "I've never seen anything quite like them before. What kind of flowers are they?"

Rich, getting a little misty-eyed, replied slowly, "Those are what you call the Magnus Begonia, and they're pretty rare. Funny thing about them is that they actually bloom at night. I encountered them while studying at a monastery in southern Tibet many years ago."

"They're beautiful. What a beautiful way to honor your wife." I could tell he didn't want to talk about it as he got up from the cedar bench and resumed his quick pace along the shore. Meanwhile, Beau lived up to his reputation and was indeed watering all the trees along the trail.

"Anyway, Jack, this isn't about me. It's your time, and I want to make sure you get everything Coach expects. The next thing you want to do is dress in a way to reflect well on the work you do. Regardless of where you are going, being slightly overdressed is better than being slightly underdressed. Remember, you're in the business of first impressions. You ever notice when you're in the airport there's one particular class of men who all wear neckties?"

"Actually, now that you mention it, Rich, yeah. The airline pilots all do."

Rich slapped his hand to his knee and said, "Bingo! You got it. Aren't they sharp and professional looking?"

"I guess so," I answered, never having really given pilots and neckties a thought.

Rich retorted, "You guess so? Would you feel more confident in their abilities if the pilot of your 747 from Philadelphia to Los Angeles showed up at the gate wearing blue jeans and a Budweiser t-shirt? I know I wouldn't get on that plane!"

"Now that you mention it, I can appreciate that."

"Does my wearing a necktie inspire visitors and members of my congregation to have more faith in my message or my professionalism? I don't know for sure, but it very well might. If you want people to put their faith in you, Jack, it starts with looking the part."

So that was lesson three: look the part. As the two of us reached the final turn along the shoreline, I realized I had a lot more to learn than I thought when the week began.

"If you fall, hit your head on a rock on your way out of here today, and forget everything else, remember this one thing, Jack. Know when to shut up. I've found that most preachers, teachers, and leaders just don't know when to shut up. Better to have a good message than a long one."

I laughed, remembering that J.J. Andrews had given me similar advice earlier in the week. I told Rich about that meeting.

"J.J.'s a smart man, Jack. He didn't get to where he is today by being a smooth talker; he got there by being a smooth listener.

"How many times have you been to church when the preacher got the sermon off to a great start and had you all fired up through the middle of it? You're thinking this is perfect, this is it, you've got us hooked, end here now! Only problem is, he doesn't. Right when he should have ended on a positive note he just kept on going, belaboring point after point?"

He had me there, and I admitted it. "More often than I'd care to count, Rich. It's why I don't enjoy most church services. I actually feel a little guilty about it, but I should tell you I haven't been to church in years. I'm a little ashamed to confess that."

"No need to be ashamed, Jack. That's precisely my point. You might have enjoyed church just fine if the pastor was entertaining and knew when to shut up, right?"

"Absolutely, Rich. I would add that you just described most meetings at people's jobs, too."

"Jack, that's why we need folks like you—coaches. Coaches aren't just for student-athletes; everyone needs a coach in life. I have a coach I work with on my message to the congregation and how to keep them involved and engaged.

"I've found it so effective that we now offer life coaching as a complimentary service to members of my congregation as well. It's really where most executives go wrong. They think because they're at the top of the pyramid they have all the answers. Well, the answers, unbeknownst to them, are right underneath their noses but are invisible to them. This is the power of an outside voice.

"I'm sure Coach has told you that you're not just coaching lacrosse, you're coaching people. You are coaching these guys to be ready for the rest of their lives, to be better husbands, employers, fathers, and friends. Lacrosse, well, lacrosse is just the vehicle. You're really in the people business."

Recalling how much I'd already learned from Coach in a very short time, I said, "He's actually shown me more than told me, but, yes, I've been learning that from him."

As we completed the loop around the lake and approached the gravel driveway to Pastor Rich's house, he reached into his pocket and handed me a coin about the size of a silver dollar. On its face were the words:

"Keep your mind on things that are true, honorable, right, pure, and respected. If anything excellent and worthy of praise, think about those things."

As I flipped it over, I saw Philippians 4:8 in large print at the center of the coin. "I should know, Rich, but what does this mean?"

"It's a Bible verse that my grandfather shared with me when I was a little boy. The funny thing is that it got my attention and interest at a time when I had no interest in organized religion. During my teen years and in my twenties, I kept this verse in front of me at all times. I would meditate on its meaning as I experienced my life's journey.

"Then when I entered the ministry in 1972, I began sharing this favorite verse of mine with members of my congregation, visitors, and friends. As time went by, I began noticing that this simple passage is really the key to peak performance in anything. When people I counsel apply this verse to their daily lives, their spiritual journey, their parenting, their marriage, and other aspects of their life, their results begin to amplify.

"So I share this coin with you because it's my hope that it will impact and touch you as deeply as it has me. What you think about, you bring about, so keep your mind focused on the right things."

"Thanks, Rich, I'll keep it in my pocket as a reminder. I'd like to stay in touch with you and seek your counsel as a mentor in the future. May I?"

"Absolutely, Jack. Like I said when you showed up, my door's always open."

14

THE DEBRIEF

After 3 days of learning at the feet of what I began to think of as the masters, I was ready to return to campus.

Like always Coach was already seated at his desk when I arrived. "Well, well, there he is. You survived. How did it go with J.J., the Colonel, and good ol' Rev?" he asked.

"The experience wasn't at all what I expected, and I mean that in the best way possible, Coach. I knew I had a lot to learn. I just didn't realize how much they could teach me coming from such completely different fields."

"Fundamentals are fundamentals, Jack. They really know no boundary," a response that sounded like the kind of answer Luke Skywalker would get from Obi-Wan Kenobi in *Star Wars*. And like Obi-Wan's wisdom, Coach was spot on.

"I knew you had a reason for me meeting with them. I just got way more out of it than I expected," I said. "You're right; there really are some universal principles about performing at a high level in anything."

"I like to call them the Xs and Os of success," Coach replied while twirling his whistle and lanyard around his index finger. "I can teach you what you need to learn about coaching. I'm so old, when I first started out the Dead Sea was just sick. So I've probably forgotten more lacrosse than most people will ever know, but you need to understand things from a broader perspective. So my thought was why not expose you to three people who could share some of their genius with you."

"I like that, Coach. I like that a lot. I guess I've just been so focused on learning the coaching business that I never thought to look outside for ideas."

"Jack, 99 percent of the workforce in every industry does exactly that. They follow blindly in their own little world like sheep in the pasture. On the other hand, the 1 percent realize that the best ideas are found outside their industry. For example, did you know the inventor of roll-on deodorant got the idea from studying how ballpoint pens are manufactured?"

"But, Coach, what exactly do the 1 percent know that the rest don't that leads them in that alternate direction?"

"It's their passion, Jack. They follow their heart, and their passion creates an intellectual curiosity. This curiosity overrides any fears and drives them. Most people won't be receptive to new ideas or explore another industry because it's outside of their comfort zone. They're intimidated because they don't know enough about that other industry; it's an unknown to them. They let their fear of the unknown keep them insulated in their little world, and they can't get out of their own head."

I could understand clearly what he meant. "We really do see that all the time, don't we? Without mentioning any names, it's like that professor with chalk dust in his hair who hasn't stepped out of the classroom in 20 years and is afraid of what he might find if he did."

"Great assessment, Jack. Guys like you and me; I'd like to think we're in that other 1 percent. We're curious. We run through our fears."

Sitting back in his chair, Coach appeared about ready for some timely advice. "I've been meeting with Colonel Duncan, J.J., and Pastor Rich for years, Jack. They are some of the brightest minds you'll ever meet. Each month I get them together, and we have a mastermind session to discuss our goals and how we can help each other. I call them the three wise men. For me it's kind of like the equivalent of having lunch with Socrates, Thomas Edison, and Steve Jobs all at once. Three brilliant minds, and I get to learn from them. So do you now. I think you'll find that just by your association with them you'll change your thinking."

As Coach talked, I knew my transformation had begun. Thinking of how each of them encouraged me in their own way to develop a philosophy and have that intellectual curiosity.

"Point to yourself, Jack."

"Huh?" I replied, a little confused by his request.

"Go ahead, point to yourself."

As Coach asked, I made a fist, held my thumb up, bent my elbow, and pointed to my chest.

"Did you notice you pointed at your heart? You didn't point to your head or your foot. That is what we're trying to get you to do, Jack, follow your heart. Great leaders like the three wise men you've just met lead with their heart, but at the same time they don't take things personally."

"Easier said than done, Coach."

"Business and sports have their good moments and their bad ones, too. They kinda mirror life in that regard. You wanna see how most people handle it?" Coach asked as he stood up and reached for a lacrosse ball on his desk.

"Of course," I responded.

Stepping away from his desk and out into the hallway, he began bouncing the ball on the marble floor. "Jack, life is like this ball. Sometimes there are highs." He bounced the ball and caught it over his head. "And sometimes there are lows," he explained as he bounced the ball down by his knees. Then he repeatedly bounced the ball at about waist height. "But there's a lot of in between.

"Here's how most people approach life, Jack. They get all caught up in the emotion of everything. When the ball's up, they're up," he said as he bounced the ball over his head and jumped up to try and catch it at its highest point. "Then when the ball is down, they're down." He then rolled the ball across the floor and bounced it off the baseboard as he crouched down on all fours to grab the ball off the ground.

"You see when the ball is up, they're up. But when the ball is down, they're down, too. That's a horrible way to live, Jack. You're just bouncing up and down from one moment to the next and allowing someone or something else's momentum to control you."

"You mean up and down as in happy and sad, right?" I interjected.

"Yes. But here's how the best of the best–guys like J.J., Colonel Duncan, and Pastor Rich–operate." Coach bounced the ball as hard as he could off the marble floor between the two walls in the corner. The ball shot up back and forth between the corner of the walls and his desk for what seemed like forever. He then just took three giant steps away from the ball, pointed at it, and said, "Look at that ball having a rough time of it today. Glad I'm not that ball."

Coach was great at illustrating his points. They were incredibly clear, both on the field for the team and right here, right now for me. "So I take it what you're saying is they don't judge things?"

"You can call it that. I call it refined indifference. They are aware of the situation but deliberately do not allow themselves to get too emotionally attached to any outcome. They don't label experiences in their life as good or bad.

"When you label failure as bad, you cut off any learning opportunity. They view failure as positive feedback. Why? Because they aren't competing against other people, they only compete against their own standard of excellence. I'm still working on that one myself, partner."

"I can see why. As coaches we're accustomed to having everything we do measured on a scoreboard and in two columns, wins or losses." I said skeptically.

I seriously doubted I could come around to this way of thinking after having the majority of my life measured on a scoreboard. From report cards as a kid, to the SATs and the scoreboard on the field in high school, to the depth chart and scoreboard in college. Not to mention my grade point average and GRE scores to get into grad school. It felt like endless comparisons, wins and losses.

"When it comes right down to, it Jack, everything is a learning experience, not a win or a loss. You are not a winner or a loser.

Think of yourself as a winner or a learner. Loss and failure can be great teachers if you let them. If it helps, consider yourself a student; that shouldn't be too hard to do around here. Life is the curriculum, and everyone you meet has a lesson to teach. Once you learn one lesson, you advance to the next."

Coach once again had given me a lot to think about and what felt like little time to do it. Tomorrow was the official start of the spring season.

"I can see how this perspective has served them well. It does seem like the difference between being good and being great. Thanks again for making those introductions, Coach."

As our conversation concluded, the more I reflected, the more I could feel in my heart that these meetings Coach sent me on were really an opportunity for self-discovery as much as they were a once-in-a-lifetime opportunity for professional development.

15

HERITAGE, HISTORY, AND TRADITION

The team veterans were familiar with day-one protocol and appeared to never tire of it. The first day of spring practice each year began with Coach addressing the team about the history and heritage of the game. It was mainly an indoctrination of sorts for the freshman and transfer recruits.

To illustrate his points the Coach brought out his handcrafted Native American lacrosse stick. It was a symbol not only of the heritage of the game but also of the Coach's longevity. The stick was a keepsake given to him by the father of one of his former players from the Onondaga Native American Reservation just outside Syracuse. What made it special was that he crafted it by hand for the coach.

"The wooden stick has a great deal of significance," he always explained. "The Native American people view lacrosse as the creator's game, and they play the game to honor God, the creator as they call him. The stick itself reminds me of mother earth. The wood reminds me of the woods, and the buckskin sides remind me of deer or moose, again from mother earth. When I go out to practice, I try to remember to respect the game because it's the creator's game.

"Did you know when Native American boys are born, they have a stick placed in their crib, and when they leave this earth, they leave with a stick?"

This was a rare glimpse into Coach's spiritual side. Usually the taskmaster at practice, his sharing the history and heritage of the game revealed a different side of his personality to the entire team.

I was in awe. I thought I knew a fair amount about the game. In a quiet moment, as we watched the players take turns experimenting with the wooden stick, I turned to Coach. "I had no idea Native Americans attached such significance to the stick. I mean, I knew they created the game, but I didn't know everything you just talked about."

"No offense, Jack, but I'm not surprised. The tradition tends to get lost in the game of lacrosse, especially at the collegiate level. There's so much meaning behind the stick to the Native American people. The traditional wooden stick just feels different. There's an energy to it, and when you hold it, it brings a different meaning to the game."

Before Coach brought the stick out to practice, players would see it on the office wall and think things like, "heavy, antiquated, difficult to use." After Coach brought the stick out to practice, demonstrated his accuracy and shooting prowess, and discussed the meaning behind the stick, players would now see the art, craftsmanship, history, and tradition behind it.

History and respecting the game were important lessons that didn't just take place on day one and then get put on a shelf for another year. It was part of the curriculum with Coach. He even scheduled an annual return to his roots and the roots of the game by bringing each of his teams to participate in the Brookhaven Lacrosse Pow Wow. The event was a nationally known, invitation-only tournament on eastern Long Island that was part of a Native American cultural festival.

His message to the team at the beginning of the season was simple and embodied authentic leadership. Coach would demonstrate everything he taught to the team. From seemingly simple things like how to put on their game socks and lace their cleats to how to properly set a pick and cut to the goal. The tradition extended to knowing who wore your jersey number before you, what their legacy was on the team, right down to what they are doing post-graduation.

There was a clear and apparent reason why when many teams placed their last names on the back of the jersey, Coach never did. Instead the concept Family occupied that space. The team was to be a family. He wanted you focused on playing for the name on the front of the jersey, not your own name on the back.

Coach was a master at connecting meaning and purpose to the players' experience from the first day forward. In the corporate environment this is known as onboarding, and Coach was an onboarding master. Little did I know my onboarding was about to get underway, big time.

16

UNCHARTED
TERRITORY

After a spirited, high-energy practice that was marked by a handful of verbal and physical altercations, Coach huddled everyone up for a quick post-practice debrief. "Don't bother bringin' your sticks to practice tomorrow. Just show up here at 6:30 A.M. ready to work, and don't be late."

In the players' minds that could only mean one thing, a conditioning practice. Anytime Coach told the players not to bring their sticks to practice, it was usually code for "you're going to run until I'm tired of watching you." It certainly wouldn't be the first time Coach did that, but it was confusing, I thought, because it seemed a little uncalled for after such a good practice.

The next morning when the players arrived at the practice field, they were met by a charter bus parked at the entrance. Coach, in an exceptionally cheerful mood, jumped off the bus, started passing out different colored blindfolds, and welcomed everyone to step aboard. After the players were boarded, they were instructed to remember the color of their blindfold and put them on. A daylong team-building adventure was about to begin.

Unbeknownst to the team, Coach had arranged to go to a 2,500-acre private, remote wooded area adjacent to Valley Forge National Park. As soon as the bus dropped everyone off, four Humvees were on hand to escort the players deep into the woods.

Before they were allowed to board the Humvees, Coach belted out the following instructions: "All players wearing blue blindfolds have to travel together in one vehicle, all wearing white in another, grey in the third vehicle, and black in the fourth. The drivers won't help you figure it out, and they also won't go anywhere until you are grouped together correctly."

To the players it must have felt like chaos had begun; to Coach this was the beginning of some much-needed team building.

Two seniors, Jake and Todd, took charge right away. Todd shouted out, "I'm at the first Humvee. Everyone with a blue blindfold follow the sound of my voice and walk over here." Six players blindly stumbled over to him in a matter of seconds. At this point, Jake let out a whistle to get everyone's attention and yelled across the grounds, "If you have a black blindfold, walk to the whistle over here with me." As he whistled steadily, the six other members of his unit made their way over to him.

Their divide and conquer strategy was working like a charm as they then repeated the same process to get the white and grey groups to their respective vehicles. Somewhat surprisingly, to me at least, Jake and Todd had everyone arranged by color, on board their respective vehicles, and ready to roll inside of 10 minutes.

Before he released the vehicles, Coach gave the following cryptic explanation: "Your challenge is for each group to find its way back to this location after you're dropped off. There's only one rule. You've gotta return all together in your units by sundown. Good luck!"

The drivers then escorted their color-coded groups of passengers deep into a wooded forest so hot you'd need a machete to cut the humidity. As they approached the heart of the woods, the four trucks went their separate ways down various forks in the road. Moments later the players were released and allowed to remove their blindfolds. Much to their surprise, they found themselves at the end of a dead-end dirt trail, and before they could ask a question, the drivers sped off in a cloud of dust. As they were leaving the scene, each driver threw a small plastic bag containing a map and a compass to one of the group members.

"That ought to keep them occupied for a while, partner. What do you say we take this bus and grab an early lunch at my favorite hangout?" Coach asked.

As our driver, Larry, pulled into the parking lot you could hear the crackling of the gravel complaining underneath the tires of his massive bus. The light on the neon sign was out, but I had to smile when I saw the place was named The Penalty Box and touted itself as America's Oldest Grille and Sports Pub. No wonder Coach loved this place.

When we went in, I felt like I had walked into a scene from the TV show Cheers as everyone greeted Coach. The hostess promptly ushered us over to what she referred to as "Coach's booth," while other people waited in line to be seated. You could barely see the wood paneling on the wall behind what was a montage of photos paying homage to the legend.

She wasn't kidding. It really was his booth. On his side was a black and white picture of Coach going toe-to-toe arguing with a ref on the sidelines, while adjacent to me was a 16 × 20 shot of his undefeated 1994 conference championship team. Above both of them was a panorama shot commemorating the first varsity game in Radnor University history.

While we enjoyed a couple hamburgers and some frosty cold beer, I directed the conversation to how we arrived at today's destination. "What made you decide to cancel practice and do this today, Coach?"

"Jack, did you see the way they were at each other's throats the past couple days?" he asked.

"No, I just heard a couple of the defensemen and midfielders jawing at each other from time to time. I didn't think much of it at the time, until the fight broke out."

This was Coach's opening for a teachable moment. "Everything matters, Jack. Everything. What you heard were symptoms. It's a virus that's been spreading, and it finally caught your attention. But make no mistake. That wasn't just a blip on the radar screen. This is why we're here today. I actually scheduled it for today a week ago, and after yesterday's flare-ups it looks like my timing was pretty good, wouldn't you say?"

Now I was more than curious. "Why drop them off in the woods, and what's with the color-coded blindfolds?"

"It's like you said, Jack. You noticed the defensemen and middies jawing at each other. They were blaming each other for a goal they let in and finger-pointing because they haven't learned to work together under pressure. So what we've done is divided them into groups by color to force them to learn to work together."

Coach was never at a loss for savvy or attention to detail. "There are two players at each position wearing blue blindfolds and one goalie, same with the other colors." At this point the purpose of the day was becoming clearer and clearer.

"I'm not sure if you're crazy or crazy like a fox, Coach. So tell me, what's your ultimate goal with this?"

"Well, Jack, a lacrosse season is a lot like the sport of orienteering. Ever heard of it?"

"Nope. Can't say that I have."

"It's what they're doing right now. You start off in unfamiliar territory, and all you have to go on is a map and compass to find your way back to your destination."

"Coach, you have a sick sense of humor. How is that like a lacrosse season?"

"Ha ha! It's easy. Orienteering and a lacrosse season are both all about unfamiliar territory. Neither one ever really lets you feel comfortable. That just comes with the territory. Ultimately, with both sports, the satisfaction of successfully finding your way is what makes it all worthwhile."

It was another one of those ah-ha moments where the light bulb went on in my head. "I get it now. So they have to learn how to deal with adversity."

Coach put his half-eaten burger down for a moment and smiled. "Yep! And more specifically, they've gotta get comfortable with being uncomfortable. It's a part of life, no matter what you're doing. Whether it's boot camp at Parris Island, the pressure of an overtime game, or recovering from cancer, what they all have in common is that people who succeed at anything do so because they are comfortable being uncomfortable. Our guys need to learn that, and I hope today will go a long way in teaching that lesson."

It was still another example of Coach's wisdom being revealed far beyond the boundaries of the lacrosse field. This was one of those universal truths about life. Whatever changes are going on, you can expect discomfort. In order to successfully adapt, you need to learn to be comfortable with being uncomfortable. The best of the best don't just accept discomfort, they welcome it.

I let it all sink in for a moment while polishing off my longneck Old Dusseldorf. "They're going to be pretty uncomfortable, Coach."

"I know. Look out the window." The sky was an ominous charcoal grey color, and you could hear claps of thunder echoing off in the distance. "They'll return tired, hungry, sore, and mentally exhausted. And that's a good thing. They are all signs of success; as a matter of fact, most discomfort is. Think about losing weight. In order to do it successfully, you will feel hunger pains. But when you do, it means you're probably burning up more calories than you're consuming."

Looking down at my plate, I said, "I don't think we're losing much weight or feeling hunger pains here, but I'm with you now, Coach! It's the same in the weight room and on the field. The soreness you feel from working out and running is a sign that you're tearing down muscle fibers in order to build them up, expand your capacity, and grow stronger."

Coach got even more animated. "That's right. When you stretch yourself mentally or physically, it shows you're working those muscles. The key is to push past the pain and welcome the discomfort. It's real-time feedback you're moving toward your goals."

With that, Coach was ready to leave. "Let's finish up, and head back. We need to get ready for their return in a few hours."

As we headed out of The Penalty Box and onto the bus, Coach explained that we'd team-build as a staff the rest of the afternoon by setting up a barbeque together so the team had a hot meal when it completed its mission.

Just as the sun was setting over the ridge at Valley Forge, groups of players began making their way back to the rally point. Within a 45-minute window, all four groups had safely returned. They looked sweaty, dirty, tired, yet satisfied. As they finished their meal of hot dogs, hamburgers, and barbequed chicken, Coach asked the players why they thought he had them do this exercise and what they had learned.

It was just like he'd said earlier–everything mattered. You could tell by the answers he got that not only did they know what was wrong with their cohesiveness heading into today, they also knew what they had done to improve the situation.

Coach, of course, supplied some final words before everyone boarded the bus for the trip back. "Gentlemen, I want you to remember today. I want you to remember this in the fourth quarter when the game is on the line and your backs are against the wall. When we are in sudden death overtime and the other team has possession of the ball."

He looked around at the faces turned toward him. "I want you to remember this when one of your teammates is in a potentially bad social situation and you need to get him out of there. The right decision isn't always comfortable. We will be in uncharted territory at various points in the season, and if you can work together to find your way out of the middle of nowhere with just a map and a compass, you can succeed at anything."

17

THE OPENING FACE-OFF

One of Coach's many traditions was what he called the opening face-off. It was a family-style dinner that always took place at his house the night before the first home game. He would invite the parents and girlfriends of his current players as well as any former players who wanted to come. It was almost a gala event, with everybody dressed in their Sunday best.

The opening face-off also served as a de facto awards ceremony recognizing team achievements from the previous season. These awards were part of the magic and mystery of Coach's approach because he had a policy of not giving out individual awards, only awards for team achievements. Much to the disappointment of the public relations office, Coach had a strict rule on not sending out press releases on individual accomplishments, only team achievements. Some called it old school. I called it smart. He just called it part of the system, his team-building system, which was clearly an all-the-time thing.

When you walked into the Randall house, a modest colonial on the outskirts of town, the aroma of baked apples hit you immediately and made you feel right at home. His wife, Stephanie, was a mother-away-from-home to 30 or 40 boys each year. As empty nesters, Coach and his wife welcomed the activity, and several players often lived at their house during the academic year.

Stephanie appreciated having the company, especially when her husband was on recruiting trips. Coach loved being able to keep close tabs on his players and help a few of them avoid some of the temptations inherent in dormitory living. The players, many of whom were first-generation college students, enjoyed the family atmosphere. That made being away from home for the first time much easier to stomach.

The team gathering was more like a family reunion, and that was the only way Coach would have it. Family was at the foundation of all he did. Stephanie's tabby cat, Jesse, was named after one of Coach's former team captains. If anyone made the mistake of referring to Coach's black Labrador retriever, Willie, as a "dog," they were quickly reprimanded and instructed to refer to him as a member of the family. You knew Coach was serious about this because Willie's name was in the outgoing greeting on their voicemail.

After dinner, the players, parents, and girlfriends were all socializing in the living room when Coach suddenly bellowed out, "Players-only meeting in the backyard. Now." The alums just smiled because they had been there before and knew the annual rite of passage that was about to come.

Once all the players had gathered outside, Coach began, "Alright, gentlemen, take off your shoes and socks and line up single file facing the pool."

The pool was actually a huge plastic baby pool Coach filled with water for Willie. "Don't worry, Willie. I'll empty it out and give you fresh water as soon as we're done," said Coach with a smirk.

I followed the lead of some of the seniors, slipping off my loafers and rolling up the cuffs of my pants while wondering what on earth we were about to do. Was this some sort of hazing ritual or bizarre tradition from his years in the Navy?

As he untied his white suede Oxfords, the field general shouted, "I'll go first. Jack, you're next, seniors third, juniors fourth, then sophomores, and the frosh go last."

Coach stepped into Willie's pool and walked from one side to the other, then stepped back onto the grass. Not knowing what to expect, I followed. One by one the seniors did the same. When they got out of the pool, they began clapping in unison for their teammates. The progression of underclassmen followed, and the activity ended with three big claps by the entire squad.

"I've just got one question," Coach shouted. "Anyone make it across without touching the bottom of the pool?" he asked.

His question was met with a resounding "No sir!" With that he asked everyone to circle up and take a seat on the grass.

Coach crouched down on one knee in front of everyone and lowered his tone as he explained, "So, now that we've established the fact that no one here walks on water and none of us are perfect, we can deal with mistakes better on the field."

"What I mean is we cannot demand perfection of ourselves or our teammates. You can aim for perfection and hope to land among excellence. We're never gonna be perfect, and the game won't always go our way. Understand?"

Coach had a way of bringing to life real issues everyone dealt with on and off the field. He hit the nail on the head with this exercise because perfectionism is really a double- edged sword. Improving your game motivates you to get better, yet at the same time if you're working harder and don't get better, it will strip you of your confidence.

His message was taken to heart. Compete with yourself, but don't beat yourself up over mistakes. He called it his RAFL method for mistake management: *Recognize* it, *admit* it, *forget* it, and *learn* from it later. These would be words for me to live by for many years to come.

18

EVERYTHING MATTERS

Each day seemed to provide further insight into Coach's personality and what made him such a powerful communicator. Our first recruiting trip would prove no different. It gave me insights into forging strong connections with people.

Coach had us scheduled to attend a high school game in Hartsburg, Pennsylvania, and meet with two of our top recruits afterwards. I could now see precisely why on the first day I worked for him he told me not to wear a tie anymore. Hartsburg was a gritty mill town that had known very little other than hard times since the steel industry began to decline back in the 1980s. Its population had shrunk by 75 percent in the last 20 years, and the poverty level had risen to twice the state average.

People there may have lost their mill and the local Walmart, but the one thing that persisted was their passion for high school athletics. Since this was a totally new experience, the closest thing I could liken it to was that it felt like we were politicians on the campaign trail.

"Everything matters. If you forget everything else I tell you this year, remember that," encouraged Coach.

"I'm not sure I get that," I replied.

"The way they walk out on to the field, how they address their mothers when they speak to them, how hard they are playing with 2 minutes left when they are getting blown out, it all matters. Right down to what they do after they make a bad play. It all says something about who they are, not just as a player but as a person. I'd venture to say that if a young man has his shirt untucked and his equipment locker is a mess that he probably also lacks self-discipline on the field and in the classroom."

I knew that Coach could be a bit judgmental but had no idea the extent to which he actually studied people.

According to Coach, it was important to arrive early and be seated in the fan section. Most coaches there to recruit for rival schools congregated either in the press box or a distant corner of the grandstand away from parents who were all too eager to shamelessly promote their son as the next great blue-chip prospect.

"Why do you want to sit among the team's fans instead of up with the other coaches?" I asked? Climbing up the bleacher steps, we were obviously not on our way to share a bird's-eye view with our competition.

"How many of those coaches can tell you half of what the parents of a prospect's teammates can? We are on a business trip here, partner. Those coaches up there are socializing. Some of them are networking, looking for their next job instead of actually performing their current one. They should be looking for a diamond in the rough who could actually help save their job. Meanwhile, we're doing a little long-range surveillance work on the field and gathering intel about the prospects from members of their community. It's the difference between playing checkers and chess."

Coach spent a majority of the game furiously jotting notes on his yellow legal pad and happily chatting with a variety of parents. You'd have thought he was running for mayor. The two recruits we went to evaluate both struggled mightily, and Hartsburg lost in the closing moments. Despite the loss and their struggles on the field, Coach felt they were ready to play at the next level and could help us.

It didn't matter to him the other recruiters had their sights set on different prospects and Radnor had the only staff there to watch these two young men. We patiently waited until the team was released by its coaches. By this point the stadium lights were out, the parking lot practically empty, and the other college recruiters long gone.

Coach approached the two prospects saying, "Brian and Kevin, I know it's late. You're tired and ready to head home. We just stuck around because I'd like to give you something and tell you both one thing. I liked what I saw out there tonight. The heck with the scoreboard. I'm talking about the effort you both gave. You played like there was no scoreboard; that's what I came here to see," Coach said as he handed each player a large manila envelope.

Pausing to make sure the boys maintained eye contact with him, he continued, "Please read this later, think about today's game, then hang it up somewhere you'll see it all the time—on your mirror or maybe in your locker. It's important that you remember this."

He introduced me to them, we shook hands, and I explained that we'd be back in touch to arrange a campus visit.

After getting back in the car, I said, "Coach, what was in those envelopes that was so important?"

"The envelope's just a small part of tonight. First off, I wanted to see how they'd respond against a superior team. What you do when you are outmanned speaks volumes. I also wanted to see how they'd respond to me when I spoke with them after a loss. Remember, everything matters.

"The fact is they didn't play well, but I still believe they are talented players. That matters, too. It matters to them, to their parents, and to me. I want them to know I still believe in them and know they can contribute to our program. The envelope is just one way I let them know."

With that he reached behind his seat for a distressed-looking, black leather briefcase that that had obviously logged as many miles on the recruiting trail as Coach himself. He grabbed another manila envelope out of it and gave it to me. "Here, this one is for you. Read it, recite it, and remember it because truer words have never been spoken."

I couldn't wait until I got home to open the envelope. As soon as Coach dropped me off at my car, I carefully unfastened the manila envelope, revealing a piece of the Coach's personal letterhead that contained a quote entitled "The Man In The Arena" by President Teddy Roosevelt. It was an excerpt from the speech "Citizenship in a Republic" that he delivered at the Sorbonne, in Paris, France, on April 23, 1910.

> "It is not the critic who counts; not the man who points out how the strong man stumbles, or where the doer of deeds could have done them better. The credit belongs to the man who is actually in the arena, whose face is marred by dust and sweat and blood; who strives valiantly; who errs, who comes short again and again, because there is no effort without error and shortcoming; but who does actually strive to do the deeds; who knows great enthusiasms, the great devotions; who spends himself in a worthy cause; who at the best knows in the end the triumph of high achievement, and who at the worst, if he fails, at least fails while daring greatly,

so that his place shall never be with those cold and timid souls who neither know victory nor defeat."

Yet again, the right words at the right time, I thought to myself. That's the art Coach had mastered. While technically he didn't say anything profound to Kevin and Brian, the quote he shared had deep meaning they would come to understand and embrace, hopefully for the rest of their lives.

That was the aura of Coach. Time and time again in virtually every encounter his message, the right words at the right time, would transcend the situation and have a parallel to the lives the team members were building.

19

A HISTORY LESSON

The next day back at the office before practice, I wanted to show Coach that I took last night's message to heart, so I came strolling in reciting "The Man in the Arena" verbatim. It was met with a one-man standing ovation and a hug. The kind of hug a kid would get from a proud father after he hit a walk-off home run to win the baseball game.

"I have to tell you. Coach, before last night I never saw or heard of "The Man in the Arena." I absolutely love it now."

"Jack, it's not so much the poem I love as the person who penned it. Sure, it's a great poem, but it's written by an even better person. You wanna know why I like Teddy Roosevelt so much?" he asked. "He was everything a coach and a man ought to stand for. The guy was the absolute gold standard for how to live courageously. Did you know he was shot in a failed assassination attempt back in 1912?"

"No," I admitted, knowing that I was about to get a history lesson. "What happened?"

"While he was campaigning in Milwaukee back in 1912, he was shot by a local saloon keeper. He didn't let that stop him though. Teddy gave his campaign speech anyway with a bullet lodged in his chest. After giving one of the fieriest speeches in American history, then they took him to the hospital. The doctors treated the gunshot wound but decided it was too dangerous to attempt to remove the bullet, so he carried it around in his lungs the rest of his life. That's one heck of a souvenir, isn't it!

"I use it as a reminder that I can't wallow in pity when life throws a curve. Whether that curve is a bad call by the refs, budget cuts, a broken leg, or cancer, just keep moving forward. That's the message I want to send the team. You've got to be a finisher. Whatever the endeavor, finish it."

"Be a finisher." It was more than advice; it was an example that Coach lived. That year, he had surgery on his shoulder. When he returned home from the hospital he found they had run out of firewood. He went outside, fired up the chain saw, and cut enough wood to build a log cabin, bad shoulder and all.

Setting a good example isn't simply one of the things a leader does. It is THE thing. People will follow your example way more than your advice. Put the two of them together, and you have the most powerful leadership tool in the world.

Coach had a lot in common with his hero Teddy Roosevelt. I could see why he was fond of him. Both were New Yorkers. Roosevelt was assistant secretary of the U.S. Navy, and Coach was a diving instructor and boatswain's mate in the Navy. They both also had a real "cowboy persona," and the two of them certainly did "speak softly and carry a big stick."

Beyond the obvious comparisons they were both ardent believers in transparency. Roosevelt was the first U.S. president to let the press corps into the White House, and Coach was a man of his word who always spoke his mind. Whether you agreed with him or not on an issue, you always knew exactly where he stood and exactly where you stood with him.

20

PYRAMIDS

The look on his face and his tone of voice said it all when Coach walked in the room. That's the beauty of people who wear their heart on their sleeve; you always know what's on their mind.

"Ugh, this darn place!" he muttered as he rambled into the office and slumped into his chair. I knew that voice could only mean one thing. Coach was back from a meeting with the administration. It was usually the only thing that dampened his spirits. Our record this season was mediocre at best, and that didn't even get under his skin quite like his weekly administrative meetings.

"What's the matter, Coach? Go a couple rounds with the devil?" I asked.

"You ain't kidding. For a faith-based institution, they seem to have lost the concept of servant leadership," he whispered so his colleagues nearby wouldn't overhear.

I thought I had an inkling of what he was referring to but wanted to be sure. "How so, Coach?"

"Well, I'm on this staff development committee to help improve the student experience and the culture of the university. So, they wanted our recommendations and suggestions for improvement, and I gave mine to them."

I gulped. You needed to be careful what you asked for from Coach because you always got it.

"Jack, have you seen the University's corporate pyramid diagram on the wall in the lobby of the administration building?" Coach inquired.

"Yes, how could you miss it? I've seen smaller interstate billboards."

Coach leaned forward, let out a big sigh, and said, "Exactly! They treat that thing like it's an exhibit at the Guggenheim. So at this meeting of the minds, I just explained to them that they have the pyramid upside down."

Not understanding what he meant I pressed for more information. "What do you mean they have it upside down?"

"Like many organizations, leadership operates from a top-down perspective: President at the top of the pyramid and then the leadership team of vice-presidents are underneath. They're followed by department managers, committee chairs, and directors who manage the support staff and faculty. Right?"

"Yeah, Coach, that sounds about right" I chirped.

"That worked when I was in the Navy. It's a military hierarchy, but in corporate America and education I don't think that's the best practice.

"If we really want to be a student-centered institution, we've got to be faculty-centered first because happy employees are productive ones. By turning the pyramid upside down you'll naturally become student- and faculty-centered. Right now, they have the administration and the board of trustees at the top of the pyramid. I think they belong at the bottom."

Coach was ahead of his time with this philosophy on leadership. At most institutions management thinks the employees work at the university to serve them as opposed to serving the students. Sometimes they're so out of touch with the students they couldn't possibly respond to their needs. Then they wonder why retention, enrollment, or applications are down.

As he pointed out the window where a crowd of students were walking by, Coach got a little philosophical. "You never want to lose touch with your people and what really matters to them. If you lose touch or ignore even just a couple of them, it's like throwing a rock in that pond over there. It may only be one rock, but it can cause a massive ripple effect throughout the whole pond. Next thing you know, the whole culture is soured.

"They think the pyramid is right side up, but really it's supposed to be upside down if you're doing things correctly. Follow me on this, partner. If you flip the pyramid upside down, the people at the top, who represent the majority of your community, are the students and prospective students. Or if you're a business, your customers and prospective customers.

"They are absolutely the most important people, so it stands to reason that the people who have the most consistent day-to-day contact with them should be empowered and actually put in a position to succeed. People like faculty, coaches, admissions counselors, advisors, and tutors are in essence your sales and customer service teams. If they succeed, then everyone else's success is virtually guaranteed.

"At my son's clothing company, he structured things so that sales and customer service people are empowered to remove all non-sales- related activities from their job descriptions. This frees up their time to go out and make money every day. The more customers they bring in or retain, the more money they make. The more money they make, the more money the company makes.

Everybody wins. He's got the pyramid pointing in the right direction—down."

I was blown away by his complete reversal of the typical corporate structure. "So you're saying the bottom of the pyramid ought to be management or administration, which should be supporting all of us out here on the front lines. And if they spent their time on things like visionary thinking, process improvement, and finding a way to add value to the student experience we'd all be better off."

"Absolutely. Look at our team, Jack. The players don't work for us. We work for them. Too many coaches blame their players for the loses and then turn around and take personal credit for the wins. They act as though the student-athletes play on the team to serve them when in reality we should be serving our student-athletes. The students are our customers."

I smiled, "They really ought to put a coach in charge of this joint."

He continued, "You even see it in the way a lot of people recruit. They make it all about the college, how it's grown and the amenities on campus. They act like the students and their parents ought to feel lucky to be admitted.

"Prospects aren't looking for that. They want to know how they're going to be supported should they decide to come here or how we will help them deal with the challenge of being away from home for the first time."

I knew Coach would ultimately bring the discussion back to our role as coaches. He didn't disappoint me.

"Same thing with our team, Jack. When you put yourself at the bottom of the pyramid, you never have to worry about falling out of touch with your players. It's servant leadership. It's also why I go to every building on campus every day. I eat breakfast with the students in the cafeteria, walk through the academic building on my way to the office, and read the morning newspaper in the library. You'd be amazed at the questions I get from students and what I hear from our players."

That said, Coach slapped me on the shoulder. "Well, enough doom and gloom for one day, partner. Let's get back to work. We've got games to win."

Management expert Tom Peters called it "management by walking around." Coach just called it doing his job, and he did it better than anyone. Corporations could benefit from his upsidedown pyramid and studying every customer touch point within the organization the way he did. They would look at issues like: How customer-centric is the business? How are they gathering customer feedback? What is their retention rate? Do the customers play a role in product development?

Coach was an artist when it came to this. He didn't paint a picture or just paint the players into the picture; he gave them each a brush and made sure they had a hand in painting it. That develops ownership and customer loyalty in a way few other things ever could.

21

SOWER OF SEEDS

That year with Coach Randall went by faster than any year I could recall. My father always told me the days are long but the years are short. I think I finally understood what he meant. The days turned into weeks and the weeks into months; next thing you knew the season and the academic year were nearing an end. It was all a blur of practice plans, study halls, game film, workouts, team dinners, road trips, and scouting reports. What wasn't a blur was what I learned. That was the one thing I had absolute clarity on. Every question, answer, wisecrack, comment, piece of feedback, and assorted words of wisdom were all well documented in my journal.

The games were played on the field but so much of my learning occurred off the field. Coach told me it would happen that way, and as usual, he was right. In those quiet moments in the car, sitting in the office, when we shared a meal, and sitting up late at night talking in the hotel, Coach took every opportunity to help me grow personally and professionally. I just wish I could have helped him and the team win more.

With our record sitting at 7-7, it was clear to everyone that we weren't going to see any post-season NCAA action, but we did get to play in a couple other tournaments to have that weekend-long, championship tournament atmosphere. Coach always scheduled a couple of these because he wanted the team to know what the conference championship and NCAA tournament weekend would feel like. Playing two games in one weekend on back-to-back days in the heat of the afternoon was grueling, and he wanted them prepared for it.

This was one of those tournament weekends late in the season, but all we were playing for was pride. We were participating in the Brookhaven Shootout, a college lacrosse tournament that was part of a Native American cultural festival on eastern Long Island. The organizer of the tournament, Anthony Matthews, was the head lacrosse coach at Division II–power Brookhaven University, and a one-time assistant to Coach Randall.

The opening round games were a breeze for both Radnor and Brookhaven. Both teams won their respective matches by 10 goals, which led to a collision course between the two squads in the championship round the next day. The opposing coaches wouldn't have had it any other way. It was an opportunity for them to match wits against one another once again.

The game was tightly contested from the opening whistle. Both teams went toe to toe trading goals during the first two quarters. At halftime with the score even at 6-6, Coach Randall called over to me, "Jack, start warming up Jake in the net. He's going in for the second half."

I couldn't believe Coach's move. Our starting goaltender, Gavin, was having an average game, not making any big saves but not letting in any soft goals either. The team was lackluster on offense and seemed tired on defense. We clearly needed some sort of spark. Evidently, Coach decided that number 00, Jake, a left-handed senior who grew up down the street from Brookhaven's campus, might ignite something.

I was upset with the decision, thinking it showed a lack of faith and loyalty in Gavin. He had outworked five other goalies in the off-season and outplayed every single one of them in tryouts to earn a starting position, which he maintained through 12 games. Coach and I agreed he had been a key component in our success all season. All season until now, it seemed to me, but I had to remind myself it wasn't my decision. I just did what I was asked and gave Jake a good warm-up, taking a couple dozen shots on him before halftime ended.

The second half began with us losing the face-off and Brookhaven having a breakaway opportunity. Their All-American attack man wound up with the ball alone at the doorstep of the goal, which typically results in a goal. Not today. Like a man possessed, Jake stepped out of the net and cleaned the attacker's clock before he could get a shot off. We recovered the loose ball, cleared it out of the defensive zone, and scored on the ensuing possession. It appeared we had found our spark.

Coach remained relatively silent on the sidelines for much of the second half. The momentum continued to swing our way as Jake would make big save after big save and we'd take the ball back downfield and score. This happened on the next three possessions, and we added another goal right before the buzzer. Jake didn't allow a single goal in the third quarter. This gave us some breathing room headed into the final stanza with a 10-6 lead. Randall's career record against his protégé was 0-5, and in six games this was the first lead his team ever had.

When the fourth quarter got underway Brookhaven came charging back, rattling off three quick goals in 5 minutes to close the gap to 10-9. "Time out!" Coach shouted. I knew he called time out to slow the opponent's momentum, but he asked me to run the huddle and talk to the team while he pulled Jake aside. I thought maybe he was going to substitute our starter Gavin back in the game. I made some defensive adjustments, tried to settle the guys down.

It turned out I was wrong. Coach didn't replace Jake. Fortunately so, as the closing minutes played out, Jake settled back in and made several big saves down the stretch to protect our lead as the final buzzer sounded.

After dousing Coach with the traditional Gatorade bath, the team celebrated by making a pig pile in the middle of the field. As they celebrated, Coach and I looked on. I asked, "I'm curious, what made you pull Gavin in favor of playing Jake in the second half?"

Coach put his arm on my shoulder and said, "Partner, for four years Jake has always played better coming off the bench than as a starter. I knew he'd be comfortable and play well even with the score tied. Plus the kid's got a ton of pride. Jake grew up just down the street, and his whole family was here watching him. He's got a lot of hometown pride, and I knew he wouldn't let them or us down today. All he needed was a chance to prove it."

I immediately understood Coach's thinking, but I had to admit my own thoughts. "I thought for sure when you called time out after their three-goal run and had me talk to the team, it was because you were going to put Gavin back in. Why did you have me talk to the team in the huddle?"

"Well, it was good practice for you to prepare to be a leader, but really I just wanted a quiet moment with Jake to tell him something."

Seeing the obvious question in my eyes, Coach continued, "I had him look down the other end of the field at Coach Matthews. I reminded him that he wanted to go to Brookhaven, but Matthews wouldn't recruit him and told him he probably couldn't make the Brookhaven team as a walk-on much less as a scholarship goalie. Then I told him to have fun sticking it to him! We both laughed, and he went back in and won us the game."

As it turned out, all Jake needed to hear was that simple reminder. Coach was right. Jake had a lot of pride and didn't like to be told he couldn't do something. It probably explains why he played so well coming off the bench and why he played so well against a stacked Brookhaven offense.

What started out with me second-guessing Coach ended with my learning a huge lesson. Coaching is as much art as it is science, which on this day made Coach Randall equal parts Picasso and Einstein. The art of knowing what motivated the individual and the science of how to best prepare the group.

At the conclusion of the championship game, all of the teams gathered for an awards ceremony. What made the ceremony special wasn't the team collecting another championship trophy for the trophy case; it was the recognition bestowed upon the leader. That day Coach was the recipient of an award created in his honor by the National Lacrosse Coaches Association. It was the Johnny Appleseed Award for his work expanding the game of lacrosse by starting numerous collegiate lacrosse programs like that at Radnor.

Much like Johnny "Appleseed" Chapman, who devoted his life to bringing the blessings of apple trees to new lands in the developing parts of the United States, Coach planted trees in the form of the game of lacrosse. It was touching on many levels that Coach was honored in such a way.

It's said that Johnny exuded such a peaceful spirit that both the Native Americans and the white man trusted him completely. Having traveled to Native American reservations recruiting with Coach, I know the same can be said about him. It is quite fitting that the original Native American lacrosse sticks are made from trees. Trees they plant for that expressed purpose.

Surrounded by his family, friends, and current and former players, Coach walked up on stage to accept the award, which he promptly passed off for someone else to hold. It wasn't the plaque or the recognition that meant the world to Coach; but rather its presenter, Anthony Matthews, that former assistant and now coaching colleague who, too, caught the coaching bug from his time with Coach Randall.

It wasn't until this event that many of the members of Randall's current program, me included, were truly aware of the depth and breadth of his impact on the game and its growth. Coach had built seven college programs from the ground up over the course of his career— seven more than most coaches build in a lifetime.

During the bus ride home, I was more than a little curious, so asked Coach about his coaching stops over the years.

"The game of lacrosse was invented by the Native American people, and they have a philosophy that they do not think only of their own survival. Each new generation is responsible for ensuring the survival of the seventh generation. That's the philosophy I let guide my career decisions. I didn't always choose the school offering the best compensation or with the greatest upside potential but the one that would enable me to build something from scratch and help grow the game. Does that make sense?"

It almost made too much sense as I began contemplating how different society and particularly corporations would all be if they embraced Coach's Seventh Generation career philosophy he learned from the Native Americans.

I could tell this topic really struck an emotional chord because he became silent and was no longer looking at me. His gaze was fixed out the bus window looking off in the distance at Long Island Sound as tears began to flow down his right cheek. Several moments later he reached in his pocket for a handkerchief and restarted the conversation.

"I'm sorry Jack, didn't mean to space out on you there. I just get a little emotional thinking about this afternoon. It's all a little overwhelming, you know? You and the team have no idea how much being recognized the way I was today truly meant to me."

"I think I do now, Coach, but it sounds like there's more you want to tell me." I prompted.

"There is. During my last recruiting trip up to the reservation, I had the opportunity to meet with a tribal elder and spiritual leader, Sike Red Hawk. We were discussing this Seventh Generation philosophy. He said to me, 'Morgan, what you're doing is important. Our work on this earth is all about planting seeds. It's about the big picture, not just our individual lives.'

"That's when I really began to grasp the magnitude of what I've been doing for the past 42 years, Jack. I hadn't given it that much thought before. I never thought that one of the men I hold in highest regard on this planet had taken notice of what I'd been doing, much less made the connection to his Native American philosophy."

"That's fantastic, Coach. What else did the two of you talk about?" I asked.

"He reminded me that everything and everyone of us has a spirit and we were brought here by the creator. They call the creator Konkachila, which means grandfather.

"He told me, 'Coach, one of the most important challenges we have on the reservation is imparting this wisdom on the youth. The Seventh Generation philosophy is the ultimate responsibility our leadership has to the forthcoming generations. It has to be properly passed down from generation to generation to ensure sustainability.'"

Listening intently, I was simultaneously struck by this long-term thinking and also how far our society has strayed from that. "Coach, it's a great philosophy and a powerful concept of being caretakers of their people and the community. But why seven generations?"

"Well, Jack, the number seven is significant because seven generations is about the longest period of time that humans can really grasp, subjectively speaking. For example, some of us had great-grandparents when we were born. We've known our grandparents, our parents, and ourselves. We may also know our children, our grandchildren, and possibly our great-grandchildren. It's really about perspective. The seven generations are a great measuring stick of the human experience."

I'm not sure which I was more blown away by—the wisdom of this overarching philosophy or how well Coach embraced it and lived it himself.

Literally every decision the Native American people make is guided by this Seventh Generation philosophy. They ask themselves, Can this decision have a potentially negative impact seven generations from now? If the answer is yes, they do not do it. It's their north star, and the challenge with this philosophy is melding this responsibility of looking ahead with living in the moment. It is leadership at its finest.

A quiet bus ride was the ideal environment for me to engage in some reflection and some much-needed journaling. Coach was right. My coaching philosophy was slowly but surely becoming clearer and clearer. Today's events gave me the chance to really reflect and do some interior work myself, how I wanted to be remembered, and how I could ensure my decisions would be made with this same focus on sustainability.

It was one thing to say you're going to think long-term and focus on sustainability and an entirely other thing to have the discipline and dedication to actually practice it. At a time when our country has had wanton disregard for protecting our natural resources, the Seventh Generation philosophy gave me a new appreciation of Native American culture. It caused me to admire my mentor all the more. He was truly one of a select few who consistently aligned knowledge with action.

22

TWO KINDS OF PEOPLE

D o not be a seed counter. Be a seed planter." These were the words Coach leaned over and whispered to me while we sat on the bench. It was poignant that our season together was ending in the exact same place my interview with Coach began—on the game field.

The final game of the season had ended an hour earlier, but the two of us didn't want to leave the empty stadium. We didn't want the season to end because it signified not just an end but also a new beginning. I think Coach knew this. This might be one of the final pieces of advice he'd give me before I moved on to the new head coaching position I had just landed at the University of New York.

"There are really two types of people in this world, Jack—seed counters and seed planters," he started.

"Seed counters are those people who waste their time constantly taking inventory of what others get in comparison to what they do. The meter is always running for them. They're always keeping score. The sad thing is when you do that you're living life externally, judging yourself against the wrong standard. When you do that, you're always gonna come up short. Look no further than contract renegotiation time with coaches each year, expecting or really demanding a little more money than the other guy."

I nodded in agreement. "Yeah, I see people like that all the time. Their greed and negativity is exhausting, isn't it?" I said, knowing Coach had lots more to say.

"Seed planters are few and far between because they're wired differently. Seed planters live life internally, comparing their results only to their personal best. They know that true wealth is not financial. It's spiritual. Seed planters have learned how to give of themselves and add value to the lives of others. When you plant a lot of seeds, you'll reap an incredible harvest. Be a seed planter, Jack."

Coach didn't get philosophical very often, so when he did you knew he was serious.

The mentor kicked his New Balance tennis shoes off and ran his feet through the rich Bermuda grass on the field. "Your career is going to be a lot like the turf here. I learned this from our field maintenance guy, Charlie; he's been in the business for 50 years and has seen it all. Take a look at this stuff.

"Before Charlie started here, there were weeds everywhere and not for a lack of effort in getting rid of them. The physical plant department spent thousands of dollars each year to have one of those turf companies spray the field with expensive pesticides and chemicals to get rid of the weeds, but it never did any good. Charlie came on board, God bless him, fired the turf company, and inside 12 months we had a grass field that looked so good you'd have thought it was artificial turf. I asked him what his secret was. He told me, 'Quit pulling weeds, just keep planting seeds.'"

"Hmm, just plant grass seed. That's all he did?" I said cynically.

"Turns out it is, Jack. He said what fertilizing the soil and planting grass seed does is help the grass grow healthy in a way that crowds out the weeds and creates an ecosystem where it's impossible for the weeds to thrive. That's phenomenal advice for anything, Jack, not just the game field. If one of our freshmen is struggling, I just remind myself to plant seeds. If recruiting or fundraising is going slow, I remind myself to plant more seeds.

They don't always take, but if you keep planting, with enough effort you will have success."

Thinking ahead to my new job, I could see I'd better add "field maintenance" to my to-do list.

Once again, Coach could read my mind. "I've seen that place, Jack. You have to take a look inside that program when you get there and examine the soil. You've got to see where you need to feed your roster and crowd out the negative."

"That's easier said than done, Coach. They were 0-14 last year. It might take me forever. I get the feeling I got the job because no one else wanted it. If you look up rebuilding project in the dictionary, there's a picture of that place," I sighed.

"That's what I'm talking about, partner. You've got weeds in your mind, and you're not even there yet. It's not gonna take you forever, but you're telling yourself that."

"Did I really say that? Wow, if I did, I didn't even realize it. I really do need to be more positive," I replied in self-disgust.

"You know," he began, "the campus psychologist told me that more than 75 percent of what we say to ourselves is negative.

"Do you realize you have a little voice in your mind? And that little voice can have tragic consequences on your life if you listen to it. If your little voice repeats negative things seed counters have told you, you're gonna become one of them. Negative messages like: It will take forever, Nobody else wanted the job, I don't know if I can do it, I'm not smart enough, I'm not talented enough. That's seed counter talk.

"Think about it. When we allow negative seeds to be planted and then we water them with our own self-talk, those seeds turn to weeds in our life. Pretty soon they squeeze out and kill off the positive. You're going to be challenged; you'll have your critics and skeptics. Heck, I've still got mine here; it's an occupational hazard. You've just got to ignore the noise and keep planting seeds."

Easy for him to say, I thought to myself. It was nothing new for Coach Randall. After all, he had a tried-and-true blueprint for growth, having built programs from the ground up and rebuilt several others.

"Coach, I grew up in a house with a lot of negativity, so I guess it's kind of been programmed in me from an early age."

"Jack, you have the ability to deprogram all of that. So don't be concerned with how many seeds are in your apple. Be more concerned with how many apples can be in your seeds. What are the possibilities there at the University of New York? People didn't think Radnor had any potential when I took the job. Early on I had recruits the admissions office told me weren't college material, and they've graduated with honors. They're now leaders in education, business, law enforcement, and the military."

"So, Coach, what you're saying is being a seed planter is all about the process."

"That's right, Jack, and when you're passionate about the process, it makes the outcome pale in comparison. But here's the kicker; the process can be long. I mean really, really freaking long."

"How do you know you're on the right track if you're not seeing results and the process takes so much time?"

"Jack, you've got to trust the process. Think about the ammunition you're armed with, stuff you got from J.J., the Rev, and the Colonel. That's your process. It works in every walk of life, and it will work for you. Let me share a secret with you. It's what I call my focus phrase.

"Remember I told you we all have a little voice in our heads that we listen to. Well, I've found that if I talk to myself and program my mind with the right words, the focus phrase, then I'm a lot more positive and productive. The focus phrase I've used for 42 years to help me keep the faith is 'Watering Bamboo.'"

All I could say was, "Huh?"

"My mentor Coach Rich Williams told me about it, and I'm gonna tell you," he started.

"Giant timber bamboo farmers plant their seeds 6 feet into the ground and water them every day for a year. What do you think happens after a year?"

"It sprouts," I answered.

"Nope, Jack, nothing happens. So the farmers continue to water the bamboo every day the next year and what do you think happens after year number two?"

"After two years, it must sprout," I said emphatically.

"Uh, no. Again, nothing happens. Every day during year number three the farmer keeps working his process watering the bamboo, and lo and behold, what do you think happens at the end of the third year?"

"Well, this is obviously a trick question, so I'm gonna say nothing happens, Coach."

"You guessed it, partner, not a darn thing happens. But they keep watering every day for a fourth year, and after four years the bamboo shoots up out of the ground at a rate of over 90 feet in 60 days."

As we laughed together, I turned to him. "I guess God teaches us a lot of lessons through nature." As I said this, I couldn't help but think back to my time as a college athlete. Four years of watering reminded me an awful lot of when I started out as a quiet, under-sized freshman student-athlete who eventually grew into a senior leader.

Once again, Coach turned serious. "It hasn't been four years, but you've sure matured a lot since we've met, Jack. I think you're ready for your next career step and will make a great head coach. The University of New York will be lucky to have you."

"Thanks, Coach. You have no idea how much your support means. You've been like a father to me. Ever since my dad died, I've felt a huge void in my life, and I want you to know that since the day I met you that void feels like it's been filled."

"The feeling's mutual, Jack, and I speak for Stephanie as well when I say this. Our kids have been grown up and moved away for a number of years, but we haven't gotten used to being empty nesters. You've become like family to us."

Coach was a big hugger, and as I reached out to shake his hand, he pulled me in to give me a big hug. I should have known better than to just shake hands.

Then the conversation ended with him saying, "I'm not big on good-byes because it usually means you're not going to see the person again. So let's agree right now we're gonna stay in touch. Our hearts, our home, and our dinner table are always open to you, Jack. Remember that, okay?"

"You got it, Coach. I promise not to be a stranger."

After I got home from the game, I decided to take the dog for a walk, and in the quiet of the night my thoughts turned to how it all started. From that fateful day I met Ben out on the field, all the way up through my conversation with Coach on the bench after today's game. I was definitely at peace with the fact that I made the decision to pursue a career in coaching. His words today really stuck with me.

We live in an instant, on-demand society, and that includes how people feel about results. They want them and expect them yesterday. If the service at the McDonalds drive-through takes too long, we get annoyed and threaten to go to Burger King next time. If a CEO doesn't provide an instant turnaround of the company, he gets the boot. NFL coaches are fired just a couple games into the season if they aren't delivering wins. Even colleges at the non-scholarship level are starting to expect instant results from coaches.

In just about every industry there has come to be a quick-results mind-set in what is naturally a slow-paced and process-oriented world. Rome was not built in a day. Coach's watering bamboo philosophy is a great reminder that the bamboo plant didn't simply lie dormant for four years and suddenly experience exponential growth after four years. It was slowly but surely growing underground, cultivating a strong root system that would support its outward growth over time. Without that unseen foundation, life above ground would be unsustainable for the giant timber bamboo plant.

It's really no different with people. I got the opportunity to learn from Coach and the leaders he introduced me to that the root system is your character, and by patiently building the character of your people, you prepare them to be resilient in the face of adversity because a strong foundation has been built. That foundation helps you handle the trappings of success and failure. If you try to take shortcuts, and many leaders do, what may appear to be instant success is really just a house of cards because it was not built on a solid foundation.

Coach made a career of planting seeds and building foundations one college, one program, one human being at a time. Many people are seed planters. They just do so unconsciously. Coach was very conscious of it, very intentional in his approach. It was just how he was wired. Some might say it was his DNA.

He took young men that many gave little chance of succeeding and created a nourishing environment where they could grow to their potential. Looking back on my time with him, I know this because I was one of them.

Coach's affinity for apples and his receipt of the Johnny Appleseed award make his statement such an apt metaphor for career success. It spoke to the people in his life that he invested energy in. His constant watering caused those around him to become strong of mind as his thoughts and actions took root, grew, and became a part of them. That was the art and science of what Coach did so masterfully.

My goal was to do as he did. To develop an unparalleled sense of humor, an uncanny ability to both identify and develop talent others could not see, and an undeniable vision for growing the game and in the process growing young men into leaders. This I hoped to be my legacy.

23

LEAVE A LEGACY

I could hardly believe what they were about to pay me to be a head coach. To put things in perspective, I kept telling myself I was being paid to go find kids and teach them how to play a game. How ridiculous was that? Little did they know, I'd have taken the job for a fraction of what they offered on the contract I had just signed.

After a morning of new employee orientation across campus, I walked back to my office at the University of New York. Betty, my secretary, was kind enough to have sorted and left all my mail on my desk. Among the recruiting questionnaires, inquiry letters, and equipment invoices was a small cardboard box. It was way too small to be lacrosse equipment, and there was no return address.

When I opened it, I found an even smaller wooden box, the shape of a cigar box. An envelope immediately fell out and landed in my lap. Resting carefully inside the box I discovered an old-school metal whistle and lanyard. The whistle showed its age with several rust marks along its edges. The lanyard was a faded piece of white nylon that like the whistle had clearly seen better days.

My office overlooked the indoor track in the university field house, and as I held this mysterious old keepsake, I was distracted by the sound of our track coach's whistle and glanced out to see the men's relay team training with him.

When I opened the envelope, I immediately recognized the unique looking Native American lacrosse player in the top left corner of the letterhead. It was a handwritten letter from Coach.

The letter read:

Jack,

Congratulations on your new beginning. I couldn't be more proud of you. Apply the knowledge and leadership skills you've gained, mentor and treat your new team like family, and I know you will enjoy a rewarding career as a head coach.

Enclosed you will find a whistle. It's older than me, if you can believe that, so you probably won't want to put your lips on it but you must keep it. I'm passing it down to you as it was passed down to me by my coaching mentor Richard N. Williams. He won 396 games and wore that whistle for every single one. When I left his tutelage in 1954 to become a head coach myself, he passed this whistle down to me and explained that he was saving this whistle to give to someone whom he felt would leave a lasting legacy. His only request was that I do the same with it one day. Please continue the tradition.

Wear the whistle, leave a legacy, and pass it on.

Respectfully,

Morgan Randall

As I put the letter down on my desk, my gaze turned back to my office window and track practice. I could hear Coach Daniels explaining to his team that the 4 × 100 relay was often won in the exchange zones. All things being equal, the team that passes the baton most efficiently will win. He then broke them up into groups of four and had them practicing their exchanges by running from the acceleration zone into the exchange zone. He coached them that after seven steps the receiver must bring his elbow back and then reach back, fully extending his arm behind him to receive the baton. Proper technique dictated that you don't look back when receiving the baton.

It was at this point, as I heard Coach Daniels shouting, "Don't look back! Don't look back!" that I realized the significance of what was in the box. As I put the lanyard around my neck in anticipation of heading out to practice, it struck me that by handing down the whistle Coach Randall was figuratively passing the baton to me. Our exchange zone was that time out during the Brookhaven game when he handed the huddle over to me. I had hit my stride and was now taking the baton and charging full steam ahead with a new team and a new season of life.

I still wasn't sure I was ready for the leadership responsibility of being a head coach. He was more certain of it than I. At this moment I realized the advice I heard coming from down on the track was meant as much for me as it was for his runners. Don't look back, don't look back. There would be a time and a place to do so. This just wasn't it. The whistle was my baton, and it was my time to run the race.

Wearing the whistle, I grabbed an old wooden Native American lacrosse stick and headed out to meet my new team at the stadium for our first practice. Unbeknownst to them, they would be getting a history lesson.

24

THE PHONE CALL

Several years later, after a long spring day had drawn to a close, I was sitting in the office planning my summer schedule. Only now I wasn't a coach scheduling trips to recruiting showcases or home visits with prospects. After 12 rewarding years coaching college lacrosse, I had moved on to become an executive coach. I had married and started a family—in Maine of all places. My wife and I were raising our own kids now instead of 30–40 college kids each year. I had always wanted a family because of the way I saw Coach with his own family as well as his enormous extended family.

Being an executive coach was different, yet the same, and I felt I never really left coaching. My recruits may have changed to corporate leaders, but it was still the same game, the business of winning. Coach Randall prepared me for this job every bit as much as for my lacrosse coaching career. It was a lesson I learned the day he had me flip open the dictionary: Teaching is coaching, and coaching is teaching. They both "provide instruction."

My scheduling was interrupted when the office phone rang. On the other end of the line was a former Radnor player, Todd, one of our team captains the year I'd spent with Coach. It was the type of phone call you never want to receive. Todd was calling to let me know that Coach had passed away the night before. He went peacefully in his sleep in his Spartanburg, South Carolina, home after finally losing his battle with cancer.

We had all kept in touch with Coach over the years and knew about his battles with the disease. We figured like anything else Coach encountered, cancer didn't stand a chance. He was too strong. Having beaten the illness twice, this was not the outcome anyone expected. We both mentioned that cancer had to take him in his sleep because if Coach were awake he would have put up a fight that cancer couldn't have won.

I had my secretary book me on the next flight to Spartanburg. Todd and I made our travel plans to meet in Spartanburg the day before the service and catch up on old times as Coach would have wanted us to. Really, Coach would have reprimanded us that we fell out of touch and should be ashamed that we had to use a funeral as an opportunity to reconnect. I felt sick about this and about Coach's passing. I knew better than to let life and work get in the way of what mattered most, relationships. Our mentor had taught us better than that.

At 6 A.M. the next morning, I boarded Southwest Airlines flight #1328 bound for Spartanburg, South Carolina. If there is one thing Southwest Airlines people are known for, it's injecting a little humor in the travel experience. On this day's flight the target of their humor was the preflight instructions. My mentors, J.J. and Pastor Rich, would have loved our flight attendant, Samantha. She was an info-tainer.

Samantha began her preflight instructions by explaining, "In the event this flight turns into a cruise, your seat cushion can be used as a flotation device." After a round of laughter by the passengers, she continued, "In the event the cabin loses air pressure, oxygen masks will come down from the ceiling. Please secure your own mask first before attempting to assist the person next to you. Unless of course the person next to you is a screaming child, then do us all a favor and put their mask on first."

I can't tell you how many times I've flown and either disregarded or not paid attention to the safety instructions at all. For perhaps the first time ever, I truly heard them; the part about securing your own oxygen mask before attempting to assist someone else really struck a chord with me. It's essentially what I hadn't been doing in my own life for quite some time.

As a lacrosse coach, I was caught up with the fitness of my team. Then later I got caught up with the health of my business. I had neglected to nurture my own health and relationships, like my friendship with Todd. Essentially, I was living in a low-oxygen plane and reaching to help other people put their masks on.

Samantha's instructions, while humorous, really made the proverbial light bulb go on in my head. Coach's death came at a time when I was already thinking about my own mortality and realizing that I needed to make some changes. I had lost touch with a friend and was lucky he made the effort to reconnect with me.

We would all benefit if we took better care of ourselves. Then we're better equipped when the time comes for us to care for someone else. My life had really gotten out of balance. I'd been working so much I neglected to keep in touch with friends like Todd, spent less time with family, and I'd become obsessed with success as opposed to significance. Coach would have been appalled.

I thanked Samantha when she passed by and used the quiet time in the air to take inventory of how I managed my relationships, including my relationship with myself. I could not and should not ever have another situation like this one with Todd happen again. We both learned from the same teacher that friends are considered family and you don't let things come between family.

Coach used to tell us that we all juggle five balls in life: family, friends, health, integrity, and work. It was a metaphor James Patterson, one of his favorite authors, used in his book *Suzanne's Diary for Nicholas*. Four of the balls are crystal, and one is rubber. When you drop a crystal ball, it will shatter, crack, or chip and never be the same again. When you drop the rubber ball, it always bounces back.

He would tell us that most people make the mistake of thinking that the work ball is made of crystal and that they can't drop it. So they let their relationships suffer and the stress of work causes their health to suffer. In reality the work ball is rubber and will always bounce back. Our family, friends, health, and integrity are the crystal balls.

When Todd called with the news about Coach, I felt sick to my stomach because Coach died, but also because I knew that I dropped a crystal ball in favor of the rubber one by falling out of touch with Todd. I was just lucky it only chipped and didn't shatter.

I put the tray table down and popped open my laptop. Self-disgust led me on a mission to type up a work-life balance contract for myself. On it I drew five circles, labeling them family, friends, health, integrity, and work. To make sure I didn't have another situation like the one with Todd, I wrote down ways I would honor each of these first four balls in my life and how I would let go of the fifth, work.

For family I would commit to having lunch with my mother once a week and spending Saturdays with my wife and kids. For friends, I built a schedule to call and email those outside the area each week and set a standing date each month for my local friends to all get together for a "guy's night," much like we did at Coach's house many years earlier. Several years and several pounds later, we might agree on light beer and a veggie pizza though.

I recommitted to my physical fitness. I had become acutely aware that the more I worked on my career over the years, the less I'd worked on myself. Armed with that realization, I committed myself to training for a half-marathon to raise money for cancer research in honor of Coach. Maybe we could save someone else's mentor's life in the process.

The integrity section was the easiest to drill down. I was sitting on a flight at 30,000 feet for one reason: I had lost my coach. Morgan Randall was a father figure to me as well as a life coach, mentor, confidante, and friend. I realized that what I needed now was to hire a coach in life, not only to help hold me accountable but also to help push me to a higher level personally and professionally. That's what coaches do. They get you to do things you don't want to do, see things you don't want to see, and have conversations you don't want to have so you can become more than you thought you could become.

The work ball was my greatest challenge. If nothing else, I know one thing about myself: I'm an intensely competitive, type-A personality, a perfectionist if you will. I would have to tackle this area of my life using a baby-steps approach. It started with agreeing to create hard, fast work-life boundaries in my life. I would end my workday when I walked in the house. Closing the garage door would symbolically serve to shut out any and all thoughts of work. This transformation would enable me to be more present with my wife and kids. There was plenty more I could work on in this area, but that would serve as a start. And starts were a good thing. Coach always liked to say, "Ninety percent of success is just getting started. It's the start that stops most people."

I emailed the contract to my wife right then with a note: Please print this out, frame it, and ask the kids to hang it by the front door. I'll explain when I get home. Love Always, Jack

I had in essence secured my own oxygen mask. Now I had to make amends with Todd when we landed. We had some catching up to do before the service.

25

REWARDS, NOT AWARDS

Former players from all over North America converged on Spartanburg, South Carolina, that week. Technically speaking it was a funeral, but Coach's family wanted this to be a celebration of his life. And everyone knew how much Coach loved a good party with family and friends.

The line of people waiting to enter the church wrapped around the building and continued down North Main Street. While I was still in shock over the loss of my mentor, it brought a smile to my face to witness a sea of team colors. Men in their forties were wearing black and gold; young adults in their twenties and thirties were wearing their team colors of white and both navy and royal blue; and Coach's current players were all sporting their green, black, and royal game jerseys.

Coach wasn't famous, but he was a legend. He was a legend among his players, former players, friends, and neighbors. While he was from the same era as John Wooden and Bear Bryant, he wasn't a famous public figure like either, and that was fine by him. He used to joke that he wasn't even a household name in his own household.

His journey reminds me of another journey from another time. There were two other people who rode to Lexington the same time Paul Revere made his famous ride: William Dawes and Dr. Samuel Prescott. Far fewer people remember Dawes and Prescott but their mission and impact were equally important. To alert citizens that the British were coming, their route involved them taking the road less traveled, the back roads to Lexington, not the main drag. Coach did the same thing; he invested his time doing big things in small places, on the back roads of college coaching, where the real work is. He realized the journey is the reward.

Most people who leave a legacy in any industry are a heck of a lot more like Coach than they are like Wooden or Bryant. They are people with big dreams doing big things in small towns all over America. The lasting effects of their work are every bit as important.

The lobby of the church was set up to be a walk down memory lane of the life that was Coach's career. Table after table of team photographs, scrapbooks bursting at the seams with 40-plus years of newspaper headlines and box scores, as well as a collection of sticks and helmets. The largest table, consuming the entire back wall of the vestibule, consisted of championship trophies, coach of the year plaques, and other "hardware" from four decades.

The amazing thing about this particular table was that Coach couldn't have cared less about its contents. The trophies, accolades, and awards meant nothing to him. What meant the world to him were the rewards of his profession, and those rewards were seated in the church. They were the relationships developed, friendships and bonds forged between the Coach and his assistants, the Coach and his players and alums.

As I reviewed the contents of this table, one thing really struck home. Life mirrors sport, and ultimately both are less about winning the actual game and more about winning the hearts and minds of those around you. This was Coach's gift. He had a way of making his players aspire to be better. Not just better athletes, but better students and better men.

As I listened to the many players who spoke at the celebration of Coach's life, I knew our mentor was looking down from heaven and rejoicing in seeing the harvest of the seeds he spent so long planting and watering. This was his national championship.

26

THE ANSWER

The funeral service itself was a beautiful celebration of Coach's life, not a time of sadness and mourning. His son Tim greeted Todd and me in the vestibule of the church with a big hug. "Jack, you look great, but take off your tie, my friend. You're way overdressed."

"Okay, Tim, I just wanted to make sure I showed proper respect for your dad by dressing appropriately at the service," I replied.

"Hey, brother, I can appreciate that, but remember two things: Dad rarely wore a tie himself, and this is supposed to be a celebration of his life, not a funeral."

As I slid off my tie and stuffed it in my coat pocket, it reminded me of the day I first interviewed with Coach and had to do the same thing. Then I began to recognize the Randall family's intentions with the service. They wanted us to be casual because Coach would have wanted it that way. We were grieving, and grief is the price you pay when you lose someone you love. While we grieved the loss of our coach, his family wanted today's celebration of his life to change our perspective. They wanted to move us from feeling sad that we lost our coach to feeling fortunate that we had the opportunity to know him. Instead of crying that the relationship ended, today we should smile and celebrate our relationship with him.

The guestbook was filled with hundreds of names, but that didn't include everyone who was there or the cards, letters, emails, and messages sent by many former players and students. The reception was an outpouring of support, love, and respect for Coach's family and the impact he had on the lives of thousands of student-athletes. While there were really no words to comfort and reduce the pain of losing Coach, it was therapeutic to share stories with so many other people whose lives he influenced in a positive way. Wives and children of his former players as well as parents of his current ones got to hear the legend of the Coach and his amazing way with people.

Coach wasn't famous by any means. He liked it that way, but he was very well known in the community. He was the recruiter who thought every prospective student-athlete should be given a chance. We couldn't begin to count the number of individuals he not only helped get into college but also helped graduate. I heard story after story from his former players. "Coach was my hero." "He was a father figure to me." "He helped me get into college." "Coach believed in me when I didn't believe in myself." "He took a chance on me when no one else would." Quite simply, Coach touched more lives than most people could ever hope to.

During the quiet of my flight home, I had time to reflect. What could I learn from this? What sense could I make from losing my mentor, a man who was like a father to me, who took a chance on me, and who was one of my heroes? The entire flight from Spartanburg to Newark I was just plain numb. On my connection from Newark to Portland, I couldn't make an ounce of sense out of it.

An announcement came over the commuter jet's speakers that the Portland Jetport was closed due to severe fog and we were being rerouted to Logan Airport in Boston at 1:00 A.M. With my car parked in Portland and no offer by the airline of hotel, bus, or cab from Boston to Portland, I befriended two of my fellow travelers to share the cost of a rental car back home. My newfound travel companions proved to be the least talkative human beings on the planet, sleeping while I drove. This turned out to be a blessing in disguise because it gave me the opportunity for additional quiet, contemplative thought. About halfway into the journey it hit me.

I'd spent the last several years honing my craft in the consulting business, reading book after book on productivity, peak performance, leadership, and team development. All of which prompted me to become more efficient and fiercely protective of my time and my schedule. I am confident a lot of other people struggle with the same issue.

It's said that some people come into our lives for a reason, some for a season, and others for a lifetime. I've had many clients who came to me for a reason, whether it was career counseling, coaching, or helping build their businesses. Many others have come to me for a season or multiple seasons. In the process I've tried to streamline and automate many of my business tasks, placing a dollar value on my time with clients. They were transactions. But at Coach's funeral I was reminded first-hand that his relationships with people weren't transactional or seasonal; they were transformational, lifetime relationships. Lifetime relationships teach lifetime lessons and how to have a solid personal foundation on which to build.

Coach didn't come into anyone's life for a season or just a single reason; he was built for a higher purpose. The last several years, I had been missing the point, but Coach was still coaching me, even at his funeral. My business was coaching people. It's not meant to be streamlined or outsourced. I needed to be taking a coach approach to everything because like him, it's my higher purpose. Fifteen years later, thanks to Coach, I had finally found the answer to his question about the two greatest days: The day you begin coaching as a career, and the day you figure out why. This was the second of my two greatest days.

AFTERWORD

This story is based in large part on the life and lessons of my real coaching mentor, Randy Mills. He was a romantic man in the sense that he loved the game, loved its poetry, and yet understood the violence of lacrosse and the viciousness of the recruiting wars. The most telling statistic about Coach is that he proved he could win in four different decades at a variety of different institutions.

Every good coach, whether it's at the level of a John Wooden or a Vince Lombardi, or at a lower level, has to be fundamentally sound. Fundamentals drive success, and good coaches coach fundamentals. A lot of coaches can teach fundamentals, but to build a successful college program and a significant career you have to have a certain charisma. Coach was charismatic, a cool guy.

When you look at the longevity Coach had and the fact that in his eighties he still presented himself as a young man, it's remarkable. It's beyond remarkable actually. It's truly amazing and it made people gravitate to him. He achieved more by focusing on a few things, things like relationships with family, friends, his team, and the game.

I think it wasn't the actual game he loved; it was the people involved in the game and the relationships he loved. Coach used the game to help his players discover things about themselves. Players learned what was truly important in lacrosse: the strength of the bond between them. Trust and chemistry won games and also hold companies, families, and marriages together.

He allowed his players to see for themselves who they really were. They learned how to trust themselves. He wasn't big on coach-speak, playbooks, or rah-rah pep talks. Instead he gave them confidence, courage, and self-awareness. His belief was that courage would teach them to trust themselves and trust each other.

The biggest lesson you could take from Coach was that lacrosse is a game where a lot of what you get out of it is what you put into it and everything else in life is the same way. He prepared young men not for just the game of lacrosse but for the game of life. His lessons taught them how to prepare for the ups and downs of life just as much as the ups and downs of a game.

He always used to tell me, "You are judged not on what you know as a coach, but for what your players learn." Coach exemplified that concept every day in his teaching, and it's a concept that is now a foundation of my teaching philosophy.

Coach made his players and assistants feel comfortable. He did so by pointing us in the right direction, letting us figure things out on our own, and staying out of the way. His rationale for doing this was that when the person succeeds, it belongs to them and they own it because they learned how to get there themselves. In the process they find out more about themselves by taking chances. These were all things completely under their control and would enable his players to become the people they wanted to become as young adults in the workforce. Coach would tell us certain things, and we wouldn't realize the significance of the experience sometimes until later in life.

That preparation for later life he provided is incredibly uncommon. This coaching philosophy of building leaders for something beyond their current experience is the exception, not the rule, in collegiate athletics. You need to look no further than the multitude of ex-college athletes who after their playing days feel lost or unprepared for the rest of their life. They reminisce about the good old days. The student-athletes Coach Mills mentored were empowered to use college athletics as a launching pad to propel their lives forward on a trajectory that led them to become leaders themselves: CEOs, entrepreneurs, military and police officers, teachers, and, of course, coaches.

Were it not for Coach Randy Mills, the opportunity he gave me, and his influence, I am certain that my life and career path would have been much different. I sincerely believe I would not be doing the work I do coaching people, if not for Coach Mills.

He was one of a kind, a larger-than-life personality. His leadership, his legacy, and the lessons learned will not be forgotten.

ABOUT THE AUTHOR

JOHN BRUBAKER is a nationally renowned performance consultant, speaker, and author. John teaches audiences how to obtain better results in business with straightforward tools that turbocharge performance.

Using a multidisciplinary approach, John helps organizations and individuals develop their competitive edge. Brubaker is the award-winning author of *The Coach Approach: Success Strategies From The Locker Room To The Board Room, Seeds of Success: A Leader, His Legacy, and The Lessons Learned* and co-author of the book *Leadership: Helping Others To Succeed.* He is also the host of

Maximum Success: The Coach Bru Show on NBC Sports Radio Boston. Brubaker was recently cited as one of *Forbes Magazine's* Top 10 Consultants Who Avoid the B.S.

His clients range from financial services and healthcare to manufacturing and nonprofit organizations as well as the thousands of executives, entrepreneurs, and sales teams from all over the country who attend his speeches, trainings, and workshops.

John is a graduate of Fairleigh Dickinson University with a bachelor's degree in psychology, and he also earned a master's degree in personnel psychology from FDU. Brubaker has completed his doctoral coursework in Sport Psychology at Temple University. For more information visit: www.CoachBru.com

APPENDIXES

Seeds of Success Resources

Visit www.SeedsofSuccessBook.com to:

- Order Seeds of Success Game Plans and Philippians 4:8 coins for you and your organization

- Print Seeds of Success posters

- Share the Seeds of Success Principles with your team and organization

- Download a Man In The Arena sign and other leadership resources

- Watch Seeds of Success videos

- Attend a Seeds of Success seminar

- Enroll in the Seeds of Success coaching program

Plant Seeds of Success in Your Organization

If you're interested in leadership, sales, and team-building programs based on the *Seeds of Success* principles, contact The Sport of Business, LLC at:

Phone:	(207) 576-9853
Email:	john@coachbru.com
Online:	www.CoachBru.com

Sign up for John's free weekly newsletter at www.CoachBru.com

To purchase bulk copies of *Seeds of Success* for large groups or your organization at a discount, please contact your favorite bookseller or The Sport of Business, LLC customer service at: (207) 576-9853.

Also by John Brubaker

"I have found that the most successful executives today manage their organizations like they were head coaches because the same qualities that make for a successful coach make for a successful executive. John shares practical insights from his coaching career to teach you how to lead with your mind and your heart. *The Coach Approach* will teach you winning strategies to bring about game-changing performance in business and life."

—*Jon Gordon, Wall Street Journal best-selling author of The Energy Bus and Training Camp*

Available for purchase at
www.CoachBru.com

Also by John Brubaker

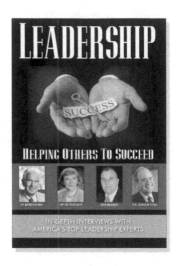

Leadership: Helping Others to Succeed is a highly successful book series from Insight Publishing. The book features best-selling authors Senator George Mitchell, Dr. Warren Bennis, and Rep. Pat Schroeder. John Brubaker, Mitchell, Bennis, and Schroeder are joined by other well-known authors, each offering time-tested strategies for success in frank and intimate interviews.

Available for purchase at
www.CoachBru.com

NOTES

Printed in the USA
CPSIA information can be obtained
at www.ICGtesting.com
JSHW022328140824
68134JS00019B/1353